1989

Mutual Fund Fact Book

Industry trends and statistics for 1988

INVESTMENT COMPANY INSTITUTE

$9.95

© Copyright 1989 by Investment Company Institute

ISBN-0-9616113-8-3

Table of Contents

How to Use This Book

The *1989 Mutual Fund Fact Book* is a basic guide to the trends and statistics that were observed and recorded during the year of 1988.

Text and Data. The Fact Book is divided into two main sections--text and data. A glossary appears at the end of the text section.

The first part of the book--text--covers basics in the history and development of the industry, key benefits and features of mutual funds, and 1988 trends in mutual funds. A series of charts, graphs, and tables illustrate some of the latest trends and help the reader compare 1988 to prior years' activity. To locate specific charts, graphs, and tables found in the text portion of the book, refer to the index on page 107.

The data section (the **blue** pages) begins with its own table of contents to make it easy to find the specific information needed. Each table in this section is clearly labeled by classification, for example, Industry Totals, Long-term Funds, Short-term Funds, etc. If you cannot find the data you need in the data table of contents, again, please refer to the index on page 107.

Data Classification. As you use the Fact Book, keep in mind that the industry usually divides its statistics into two broad categories: long-term funds (stock, bond, and income funds) and short-term funds (money market and short-term municipal bond funds). To obtain the total industry picture, refer to the notes at the bottom of the tables in both the text and the data sections (the **blue** pages). In the Long-term Funds section, for example, a note at the bottom of the page will refer to comparable short-term data or total industry data, when applicable.

The data section containing total industry statistics includes information on total industry shareholder accounts, assets, and number of funds. (This section does not provide total sales figures which would combine long-term and short-term fund sales. Due to the special nature of short-term funds and the huge, continuous inflows and outflows of money they experience, it would be misleading to add their sales figures to those of the long-term funds. Tracking periodic changes in total assets is usually the preferred method of following trends of short-term funds.)

Beginning with last year's Fact Book, the Institute further refined the industry's investment objectives by adding seven categories. The new categories are global equity, income-equity, flexible portfolio, income-bond, global bond, high-yield bond, and short-term state municipal bond--bringing the total number of fund categories to 22.

These categories have been recalculated back to 1985, so all tables involving data broken down by investment objective include only 1985, 1986, 1987, and 1988. (Prior to last year's edition, the data for these categories were included in a variety of the 15 already existing categories.)

1988: Adjusting to Change

Financial markets and the investment community faced numerous
changes at the start of 1988, many of
which stemmed from the market break
of the previous year. Adjusting to these
changes was a primary concern of both
investors and the mutual fund industry during the year.

The economy held up well in spite of
the previous year's turbulence in the
financial markets. The economy's
strength in 1988 can largely be attributed to substantial injections of liquidity by the Federal Reserve Board (the
Fed) following the October 1987 market
break. With the availability of ample
credit, the economy was able to expand
at the robust rate of 3.8 percent--an
increase in real GNP--for the year. This
was fractionally higher than the pace of
3.4 percent achieved in 1987.

Other signs of strength in the economy appeared during the year as well.
The unemployment rate fell to its low-
est level in years, ending 1988 at 5.3
percent. Industrial capacity utilization
rates rose to their highest level in more
than ten years, while the trade deficit
declined substantially. Net exports
were up 25.3 percent for the year, although this improvement occurred only
during the first half of 1988.

The positive signs for the economy,
however, did not overshadow certain
persistent problems that added much
uncertainty to the public's investment
decisions. Although the rate of change
in the consumer price index rose only
marginally during the year, fear that
the inflationary "spiral" would be set in
motion increased. These fears were

fueled by concern over the Fed's less
restrictive credit policies following the
1987 market break and a lack of
progress in reducing the federal
budget deficit. Inflationary fears were
also sustained by persistently strong
consumer demand and rising rates of
industrial capacity utilization.

The interest rate situation instilled a
degree of uncertainty in the financial
markets, which added to investors'
difficulties in charting their course
during 1988. Although both bond
prices and stock prices increased over
the year, investors were not eager to
reenter the market. A substantial part
of some of their coolness toward equities and equity products and, to a
lesser extent, toward long-term bonds
can be explained by the traumatic
experience of the October 1987 epi-
sode. Another reason for investors'
unwillingness to accumulate long-
term instruments was the changing
course of short-term interest rates. In
early 1988, when it became apparent
that the stock market break had no
discernible effect on economic activity,
efforts were initiated by the Fed to
tighten credit. In response, interest
rates rose in the second quarter of
1988. Short-term rates were especially affected, with Treasury bill rates
increasing by more than 240 basis
points from March through December.
Consequently, the spread between
long- and short-term interest rates
narrowed substantially, making short-
term debt an especially attractive
investment alternative.

Investors' concerns during 1988 are

Stock and Bond Prices

Index

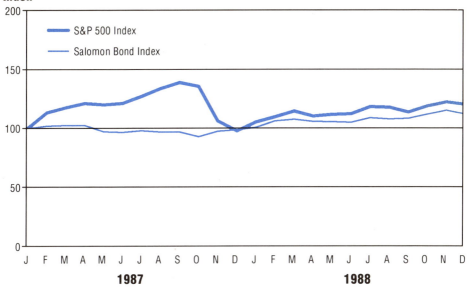

- S&P 500 Index
- Salomon Bond Index

1987   **1988**

Interest Rates
(percentages)

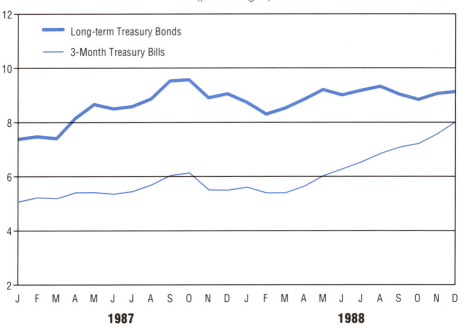

- Long-term Treasury Bonds
- 3-Month Treasury Bills

1987   **1988**

Mutual Fund Sales
(billions of dollars)

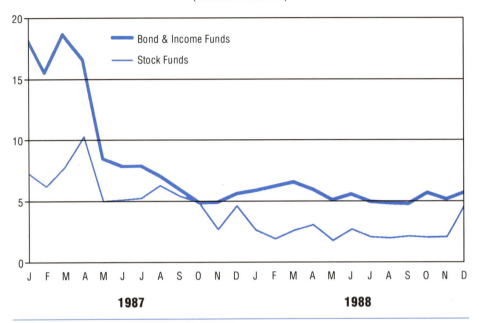

Bond & Income Funds

Stock Funds

1987

1988

Mutual Fund Total Net Assets
(billions of dollars)

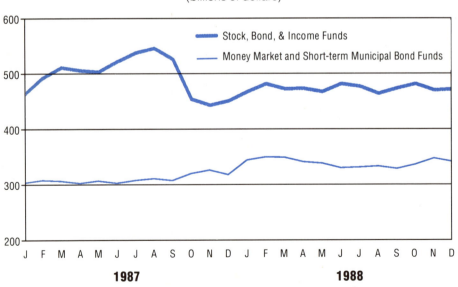

Stock, Bond, & Income Funds

Money Market and Short-term Municipal Bond Funds

1987

1988

reflected to a certain extent in mutual fund sales. After peaking in August 1987, sales of stock and bond funds hobbled through 1988 at half their previous year's level. Bond and income fund sales exceeded stock fund sales in 1988 by a ratio of just over two-to-one, finishing the year with total sales of $64.3 billion. Stock fund sales, meanwhile, ended the year at $31 billion. Even though sales were off from last year's levels, they continued to be substantially above historic trends--1988 stock fund sales were only exceeded in the two previous years and bond fund sales in the three previous years.

Redemptions for long-term funds declined in 1988 by 20.4 percent from their 1987 levels. Bond and income funds experienced a larger decline in redemptions (-24.1 percent) than did stock funds (-13.4 percent). Stronger sales resulted in net sales of over $6.6 billion for bond and income funds for the year. The decline in redemptions for stock funds did not keep pace with sliding sales. Net redemptions for stock funds occurred for the first time since 1979. Combined, however, long-term funds experienced net sales of $2.8 billion for 1988.

Total assets of mutual funds reached the level of $810.3 billion by the end of 1988. This is equal to just over 95 percent of the historic high reached in August of the previous year. Following the severe drop in assets experienced during the last half of 1987, almost $57 billion was added during the first two months of 1988. This increase pushed fund assets above the $800 billion mark where they remained for all but one month of the year.

Mutual Funds Net New Money Flow Related to Net New Money Flow from Individuals to Savings and Investment Vehicles

(billions of dollars)

Year	Net New Money to Savings and Investment Vehicles[1]	Net New Money to Mutual Funds[2]	Mutual Funds Net New Money as a Percent of Total
1960	$32.5	$1.3	4.0%
1965	59.0	2.4	4.1
1970	78.8	1.6	2.0
1975	174.4	0.5	0.3
1980	326.3	31.4	9.6
1981	353.2	109.6	31.0
1982	402.3	37.6	9.3
1983	502.6	(18.2)	--
1984	540.8	73.0	13.5
1985	543.8	88.9	16.3
1986	520.6	190.0	36.5
1987	482.7R	72.8	15.1
1988	517.9	10.1	2.0

[1]From the "FRB Study of the Volume and Composition of Individuals' Savings" as reported in the Statistical Bulletins. Seasonally adjusted annual rates of individuals' savings.

[2]Investment Company Institute reporting companies, including money market funds.
R--Revised

Short-term fund assets--both money market funds and short-term municipal bond funds--increased by almost 7 percent during the course of 1988. Money market fund assets, although up from their December 1987 levels, had a mixed year in 1988 with gains occurring in the first quarter, falling off in late spring, and then recouping by the end of the year. Increases in the early months of 1988 largely represented investors' movement to safer investments, while gains in the summer and later months were mainly induced by increases in short-term yields. Short-term municipal bond fund assets remained fairly constant for the year.

Assets for both bond and income funds and equity funds also rose for the year. Equity fund assets had an annual increase of 7.8 percent and attained the level of $194.8 billion by the end of 1988. This increase was essentially a product of price appreciation. Bond and income fund assets rose by 1.6 percent to $277.5 billion, an increase primarily attributable to new sales.

What Is a Mutual Fund?

The Basics

A mutual fund is a company that makes investments on behalf of individuals and institutions with similar financial goals.

Pooling is the key to mutual fund investing. By pooling the financial resources of thousands of shareholders--each with a different amount to invest--investors gain access to the expertise of the country's top money managers, wide diversification of ownership in the securities markets, and a variety of services otherwise available only to institutions and wealthy families and individuals.

Professional money managers take this pool of money and invest it in a variety of stocks, bonds, or other securities selected from a broad range of industries and government agencies and authorities. Money managers select securities that best meet their fund's investment objectives. These managers make the decisions on when to buy, when to sell, and when to hold based on their extensive research.

The investment objective set forth by the fund is important to both the manager and the investor. The fund manager uses it as a guide when choosing investments for the fund's portfolio. Investors use it to determine which funds are suitable for their needs. Mutual funds' investment objectives cover a wide range, from higher risk in the search for higher returns to immediate income from more stable investments. The Investment Company Institute classifies mutual funds into 22 major catego-

ries of investment objectives. (For a definition of each, see pages 9-10.)

To achieve these objectives, fund managers may invest in as many as 50 to 200 or more different securities, seeking diversification among companies, industries, and other organizations and institutions in order to reduce investment risk. The object: to avoid putting all one's investment eggs in one basket. In effect, each investor within the fund owns a proportionate share of each of those securities. When those securities appreciate in value--or pay out dividends or interest--all the fund's investors reap their proportionate share. Investors who put $1,000 into the fund get the same rate of return or yield as those putting in $100,000.

Mutual funds can make money for their shareholders in three ways. One, they pay shareholders dividends and interest earned from the fund's investments. Two, if a security held by a fund is sold at a profit, funds pay shareholders capital gains distributions. And three, if the value of the securities held by the fund increases, the value of each mutual fund share increases proportionately.

For example, if a fund's investment objective is current income, it will invest in stocks or bonds which produce current dividends or interest. Then the fund passes through to its shareholders the dividends from those earnings.

Capital gains are realized when a fund sells a security for a higher price than it originally paid. The fund usually passes that gain through to its shareholders as a capital gains distribution. (If the gain is not passed along, investors profit from an increased value of their fund shares.)

Shareholders can have dividends and capital gains reinvested in additional shares of the fund or they can have the fund send them a check for the amount of earnings.

If the securities held in the fund's portfolio increase in value, but the fund holds on to those securities instead of selling them, this increases the value of the fund's total portfolio and thus the fund's price per share.

When investors pool their money in a mutual fund, their dollars buy shares in that fund. To determine the price of these shares, at the end of each business day the fund adds up the value of all securities held in its portfolio, after expenses, and divides the total by the number of shares outstanding. Unlike a traditional corporation, mutual funds can issue an unlimited number of shares. In addition, shareholders have the right to redeem part or all of their holdings at any time.

Each day, the fund must determine both the value of its portfolio and how many shares are outstanding. That simple calculation gives the fund its Net Asset Value or NAV. Because it represents the value of a single share in the fund, the NAV is important to know when the fund shareholder is either redeeming shares or purchasing new shares.

To determine the value of their holdings, individual fund shareholders simply multiply the number of shares they own by the NAV. Although the NAV may not seem to change much over time, dividend and capital gain reinvestments can contribute toward buying many more shares than originally purchased. So even if the price of each share does not change a great deal, owning many

more of them represents an increase in the value of the shareholder's investment.

Under the Internal Revenue Code, mutual funds that observe certain guidelines serve as conduits through which the capital gains, dividends, interest, and other income flow through from the securities held in the fund's portfolio to the shareholders. Ordinarily, mutual funds pay no tax on this income. Instead, individual shareholders treat dividends and capital gains received from the fund exactly as they would had they bought and sold the securities themselves without the fund serving as an intermediary.

For tax purposes, shareholders receive a yearend statement from the fund showing clearly what part of the money distributed to them represents ordinary income and what part represents long-term capital gains. (Even though dividends and long-term capital gains are taxed the same under the Tax Reform Act of 1986, the distinction between them is maintained since capital gains can still be offset by capital losses.) Shareholders also receive regular statements from the fund that not only show them how their investments are doing, but also report on the fund's progress, its portfolio holdings, expenses, changes in management, and other relevant data.

How a Fund Is Organized

A management company may offer anywhere from one mutual fund to a dozen or more, each with a different investment objective.

When a new fund is established, it enters into a contract with an investment adviser (usually the sponsoring organization) to manage the fund and to select its portfolio. The investment adviser is usually paid for these services through a fee based on the total value of assets managed. Such investment management fees average about one-half of one percent annually. Other fund operating expenses are usually in the same range, for a total of about one percent per year for all the fund's costs of operations.

Funds may also contract with a principal underwriter who arranges for the distribution of the fund's shares to the investing public.

Fund shares are distributed to the public in a variety of ways. There are two basic avenues, however: funds that market their shares directly to the public and those that market their shares through a sales force. Funds that market shares directly often use advertising and direct mail to reach investors. Their shares are usually distributed with a low or no sales commission. In some cases, the fund's directors may authorize use of a small percentage of fund assets to support distribution efforts. This is known as a "12b-1 fee," named after the federal regulatory rule that permits it.

Fund shares marketed through a sales force are available through brokers, financial planners, insurance agents and, in some cases, through a sales force employed by a fund organization specifically to market the shares of its associated funds. These sales people can be compensated for their services to the investor through a direct sales commission included in the price at which the fund's shares are offered, through a 12b-1 distribution fee paid by the fund, or in both ways.

All mutual fund activities are highly regulated. Mutual funds must register with the United States Securities and Exchange Commission (SEC) pursuant to the Investment Company Act of 1940. The activities of mutual funds and their relationship with the public are regulated under this and other federal securities laws, as well as the securities laws of all the states where securities are sold. (See the "Regulation and Taxation" chapter.)

Types of Mutual Funds

Aggressive Growth Funds seek maximum capital gains as their investment objective. Current income is not a significant factor. Some may invest in stocks that are somewhat out of the mainstream such as those in fledgling companies, new industries, companies fallen on hard times, or industries temporarily out of favor. They may also use specialized investment techniques such as option writing. The risks are obvious, but the potential for reward should also be greater.

Growth Funds invest in the common stock of more settled companies but, again, the primary aim is to produce an increase in the value of their investments through capital gains, rather than a steady flow of dividends.

Growth and Income Funds invest mainly in the common stock of companies with a longer track record--companies that have both the expectation of a higher share value and a solid record of paying dividends.

Precious Metals Funds invest in the stocks of gold mining companies and other companies in the precious metals business.

International Funds invest in the stocks of companies located outside the U.S.

Global Equity Funds invest in the stocks of both U.S. companies and foreign companies.

Income-equity Funds invest primarily in stocks of companies with good dividend-paying records.

Option/Income Funds seek a high current return by investing primarily in dividend-paying common stocks on which call options are traded on national securities exchanges. Current return generally consists of dividends, premiums from writing call options, net short-term gains from sales of portfolio securities on exercises of options or otherwise, and any profits from closing purchase transactions.

(continued on next page)

Types of Mutual Funds *(continued)*

Flexible Portfolio Funds invest in common stocks, bonds, money market securities, and other types of debt securities. The portfolio may hold up to 100 percent of any one of these types of securities or any combination thereof, and may easily change depending upon market conditions.

Balanced Funds generally have a three-part investment objective: 1) to conserve the investors' principal; 2) to pay current income; and 3) to increase both principal and income. They aim to achieve this by owning a mixture of bonds, preferred stocks, and common stocks.

Income-mixed Funds seek a high level of current income for their shareholders. This may be achieved by investing in the common stock of companies that have good dividend-paying records. Often corporate and government bonds are also part of the portfolio.

Income-bond Funds invest in a combination of government and corporate bonds for the generation of income.

U.S. Government Income Funds invest in a variety of government securities. These include U.S. Treasury bonds, federally guaranteed mortgage-backed securities, and other government issues.

GNMA or Ginnie Mae Funds (Government National Mortgage Association) invest in government-backed mortgage securities. To qualify for this category, the majority of the portfolio must always be invested in mortgage-backed securities.

Global Bond Funds invest in bonds issued by companies or countries worldwide, including the U.S.

Corporate Bond Funds, like income funds, seek a high level of income. They do so by buying bonds of corporations for the majority of the fund's portfolio. The rest of the portfolio may be in U.S. Treasury and other government entities' bonds.

High-yield Bond Funds are corporate bond funds that predominantly invest in bonds rated below investment grade. In return for a generally higher yield, investors bear a greater degree of risk than for more highly rated bonds.

Long-term Municipal Bond Funds invest in bonds issued by local governments--such as cities and states--which use the money to build schools, highways, libraries, and the like. These funds predominantly invest at all times in municipal bonds that are exempt from federal income tax. Because the federal government does not tax the income earned on most of these securities, the fund can pass the tax-free income through to shareholders. For some taxpayers, portions of income earned on these securities may be subject to the federal alternative minimum tax.

Short-term Municipal Bond Funds invest in municipal securities with relatively short maturities. They are also known as tax-exempt money market funds. For some taxpayers, portions of income earned on these securities may be subject to the federal alternative minimum tax.

Long-term State Municipal Bond Funds predominantly invest at all times in municipal bonds which are exempt from federal income tax as well as exempt from state taxes for residents of the state specified by the fund name. For some taxpayers, portions of income earned on these securities may be subject to the federal alternative minimum tax.

Short-term State Municipal Bond Funds invest in municipal securities with relatively short maturities. Because they contain the issues of only one state, they are exempt from state taxes for residents of the state specified by the fund name. For some taxpayers, portions of income earned on these securities may be subject to the federal alternative minimum tax.

Money Market Mutual Funds invest in the short-term securities sold in the money market. (Large companies, banks, and other institutions invest their surplus cash in the money market for short periods of time.) In the entire investment spectrum, these are generally the safest, most stable securities available. They include Treasury Bills, certificates of deposit of large banks, and commercial paper (the short-term IOUs of large U.S. corporations).

Historical Background

America's mutual fund industry has enjoyed enormous success since the first fund was organized in Boston in 1924.

That fund, and the profusion of funds to follow, were an outgrowth of a concept originating in nineteenth century England. Some years later, money invested in English and Scottish investment companies (or trusts, as they are known there) contributed to the financing of the American economy after the Civil War. Investors in these British companies financed U.S. farm mortgages, railroads, and other industries.

In the early 1920s, as twentieth century America began to mature, many types of financial institutions were formed, offering Americans wider avenues for investment. Several companies, most of them located in New York, Boston, and Philadelphia, tried to meet those needs. Soon, these bankers, brokers, and investment counselors were joined by mutual funds.

Shortly after the first funds were organized, America witnessed the stock market crash of 1929. Despite setbacks, many of the efficiently managed investment companies maintained their pattern of growth and service, and the industry has grown dramatically over the years.

In 1936, under a congressional mandate, the Securities and Exchange Commission (SEC) undertook a special study of investment companies which culminated in the Investment Company Act of 1940. Industry professionals who worked closely with the SEC to draft the 1940 act decided to form a permanent committee to cooperate with the SEC in formulating the rules and regulations that would implement the new law. The committee would also stay informed of trends in state and federal legislation affecting mutual funds. This pioneering committee would be called the National Committee of Investment Companies.

As their activities increased, the committee leadership decided in October 1941 to change the organization's name to the National Association of Investment Companies (NAIC). NAIC, based in New York City, took on the responsibilities of public education, liaison with the SEC, and the monitoring of tax and other legislation affecting mutual funds, as well as exerting a strong influence to maintain high industry standards. NAIC changed its name to the Investment Company Institute (ICI) in 1961. In 1970, ICI moved to Washington, DC.

The industry ICI represents has undergone many changes since the 1940 legislation that gave it birth. At that time, there were only 68 mutual funds with $448 million in assets and 296,000 shareholder accounts. It was an industry primarily providing a way to invest in the stock market. Some funds invested in bonds, but these were not a significant force until many years later.

The industry progressed steadily until the 1970s. By then, there were 400 funds with assets of about $40 billion. In the early 1970s, a new concept signaled a dramatic change in the industry--the money market mutual fund. This novel concept let the small investor participate in the high short-term interest rates of the money market that previously were available only to major institutions and the wealthy.

The idea cracked the mold in many respects. First, new investors who had never been in mutual funds gave money market funds a try. Some had never had their money in anything but 5¼ or 5½ percent passbook accounts. Many learned the value of the mutual fund concept and, in fact, 30 percent of all mutual fund investors say their first fund was a money market fund.

Second, the money market funds sparked a surge of creativity in the industry. What followed were municipal bond funds in 1976 (achieved in the enactment of the Tax Reform Act of 1976), option/income funds in 1977, government income and Ginnie Mae funds in the early 1980s, and specialty or sector funds throughout that period. At the end of 1988, there were more than 2,800 mutual funds with assets of more than $800 billion. The industry continues to grow and prosper despite periods of market volatility, providing investment diversification and professional management to over 30 million individual investors.

Growth and Development

The mutual fund industry is now a diversified financial industry able to respond to varied investment climates and investor needs. That was not always the case. In 1978, money market funds accounted for only 19.4 percent of mutual fund assets. At the same time, equity (stock) funds held 52.6 percent of the assets.

By 1980, that had changed. Money market funds (combined with their new tax-exempt version--short-term municipal bond funds) comprised 57 percent of all mutual fund assets. Equity funds represented 30 percent of assets and bond and income funds had only 13 percent. In 1988, bond and income funds had a bigger share than equity funds: 34.3 percent versus 24.0 percent. Meanwhile, short-term funds (money market and short-term municipals) made up less than half of all assets--standing at 41.7 percent at yearend 1988. This continued shifting of assets indicates widespread investor acceptance of the variety of mutual fund portfolios now offered by the industry.

Total assets have skyrocketed in these nine short years. Money market fund assets jumped from $74.4 billion in 1980 to $272.3 billion at the end of 1988. Short-term municipal bond fund assets grew from $1.9 billion in

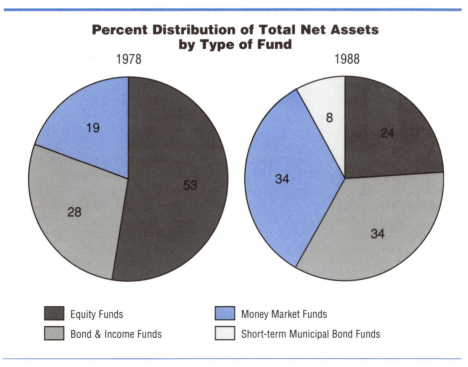

Percent Distribution of Total Net Assets by Type of Fund

1978

19

53

28

1988

8

24

34

34

■ Equity Funds   ■ Money Market Funds
■ Bond & Income Funds   □ Short-term Municipal Bond Funds

Number of Mutual Funds

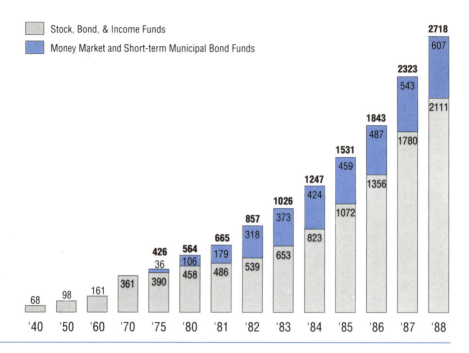

Stock, Bond, & Income Funds

Money Market and Short-term Municipal Bond Funds

Year	Stock, Bond, & Income	Money Market & Short-term Municipal Bond	Total
'40	68		68
'50	98		98
'60	161		161
'70	361		361
'75	390	36	426
'80	458	106	564
'81	486	179	665
'82	539	318	857
'83	653	373	1026
'84	823	424	1247
'85	1072	459	1531
'86	1356	487	1843
'87	1780	543	2323
'88	2111	607	2718

1980 to $65.7 billion by yearend 1988. Equity funds had assets of $41.0 billion in 1980 compared to $194.8 billion at the end of 1988. The bond and income fund category soared from $17.4 billion in 1980 to $277.5 billion at the end of 1988. Combined assets of all funds at the end of 1980 were $134.7 billion. On December 31, 1988, they were $810.3 billion.

The last few years have witnessed a shifting asset mix: from approximately 40 percent long-term and 60 percent short-term in 1983, to roughly 50-50 in 1985, to 58 percent long-term and 42 percent short-term in 1988.

Number of Funds Increases Dramatically

A substantial change has taken place over the years in the number of funds available to investors. In just one decade, the number of funds has increased over five times--from 505 funds in 1978 to 2,718 funds at the end of 1988. The increasing variety and number of funds exemplify the enormous growth that has occurred in the mutual fund industry.

In the 1950s and 1960s, the industry's historic concentration in equity funds was reflected in steep increases in sales and assets of these funds. This growth occurred in a period when stock prices were climbing steadily with only slight interruptions. However, from 1968 to 1974, a weak stock market, rising interest rates, inflation, and other economic and financial uncertainties heightened investor concern about risks associated with equities and dimmed the perception of the funds' potential returns. Consequently, investors stepped away from stocks and equity mutual funds and moved toward the relative safety of short-term liquid assets.

Mutual Fund Shareholder Accounts
(millions)

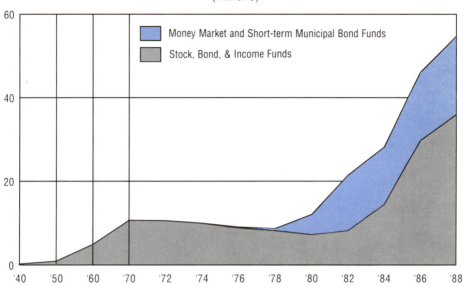

Assets of Mutual Funds
(billions of dollars)

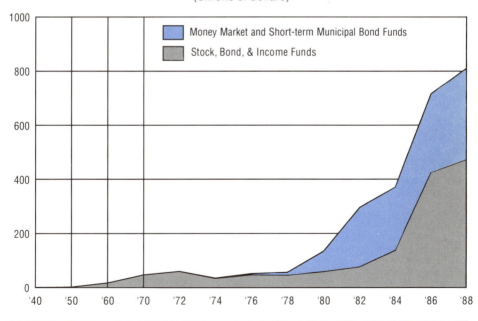

Sales, Redemptions, and Assets
(billions of dollars)

Equity, Bond, and Income Funds

Year	Sales	Redemptions	Net Sales	Assets
1971	$ 5.1	$4.8	$0.3	$55.0
1972	4.9	6.6	(1.7)	59.8
1973	4.4	5.7	(1.3)	46.5
1974	3.1	3.4	(0.3)	34.1
1975	3.3	3.7	(0.4)	42.2
1976	4.4	6.8	(2.4)	47.6
1977	6.4	6.0	0.4	45.0
1978	6.7	7.2	(0.5)	45.0
1979	6.8	8.0	(1.2)	49.0
1980	10.0	8.2	1.8	58.4
1971	9.7	7.5	2.2	55.2
1982	15.7	7.6	8.1	76.8
1983	40.3	14.7	25.6	113.6
1984	45.9	20.0	25.9	137.1
1985	114.3	33.8	80.5	251.7
1986	215.8	67.0	148.8	424.2
1987	190.6	116.2	74.4	453.8
1988	95.3	92.5	2.8	472.3

Money Market Mutual Funds

Year	Sales	Redemptions	Net Sales	Assets
1975	$6.7	$5.9	$0.8	$3.7
1975	9.4	9.6	(0.2)	3.7
1977	10.7	10.7	0.0	3.9
1978	30.5	24.3	6.2	10.9
1979	111.9	78.4	33.5	45.2
1980	232.2	204.1	28.1	74.4
1981	451.9	346.7	105.2	181.9
1982	581.8	559.6	22.2	206.6
1983	463.0	508.7	(45.7)	162.5
1984	572.0	531.1	40.9	209.7
1985	730.1	732.3	(2.2)	207.5
1986	792.3	776.3	16.0	228.3
1987	869.1	865.7	3.4	254.7
1988	903.4	899.4	4.0	272.3

Short-term Municipal Bond Funds

Year	Sales	Redemptions	Net Sales	Assets
1979	$0.6	$0.4	$0.2	$0.3
1980	5.3	3.8	1.5	1.9
1981	10.5	8.3	2.2	4.2
1982	29.4	22.2	7.2	13.2
1983	44.5	42.4	2.1	16.8
1984	62.3	55.9	6.4	23.8
1985	109.4	98.8	10.6	36.3
1986	197.5	172.3	25.2	63.8
1987	191.9	196.9	(5.0)	61.4
1988	178.3	175.0	3.3	65.7

Net Exchanges by Investment Objective -- 1988
(millions of dollars)

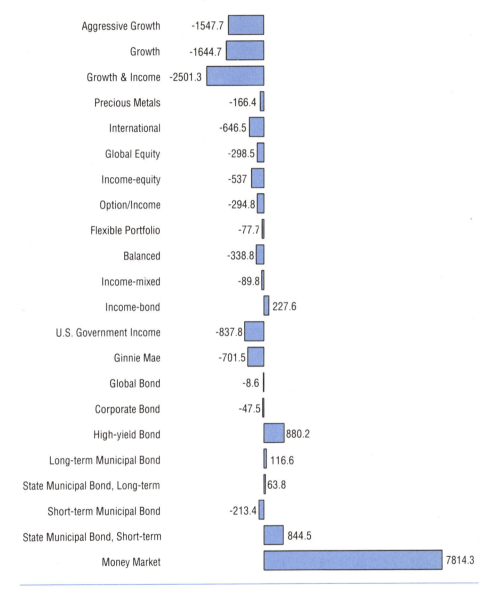

Investment Objective	Value
Aggressive Growth	-1547.7
Growth	-1644.7
Growth & Income	-2501.3
Precious Metals	-166.4
International	-646.5
Global Equity	-298.5
Income-equity	-537
Option/Income	-294.8
Flexible Portfolio	-77.7
Balanced	-338.8
Income-mixed	-89.8
Income-bond	227.6
U.S. Government Income	-837.8
Ginnie Mae	-701.5
Global Bond	-8.6
Corporate Bond	-47.5
High-yield Bond	880.2
Long-term Municipal Bond	116.6
State Municipal Bond, Long-term	63.8
Short-term Municipal Bond	-213.4
State Municipal Bond, Short-term	844.5
Money Market	7814.3

During the mid-1970s, when investor demand for equity products was declining, the industry introduced money market funds, which quickly became very popular with investors. Then came municipal bond funds, and new versions of standard stock and bond funds, such as international funds, precious metals funds, and, more recently, Ginnie Mae and government income funds. By broadening its product line and encouraging use of the exchange feature within a family of funds, the industry transformed itself into a diversified financial business capable of providing a variety of benefits to both individual and institutional investors under all kinds of economic conditions.

Mutual fund sales in the past decade demonstrate the popularity of a diversified industry. Annual sales of money market funds have nearly quadrupled since 1980, and short-term municipal bond fund sales are 34 times their 1980 level. Sales of equity and bond funds set new record levels during the 1980s, partly due to investor recognition of the excellent performance of both types of funds. Sales of long-term mutual funds reached the all-time, one-year record of $215.8 billion in 1986. The softness in the bond market beginning in March 1987 and the sudden stock market drop on October 19, 1987 created uncertainty among investors with regard to the financial markets. This in turn caused a decline in total sales of equity and bond funds in 1987 to $190.6 billion, and a further decline in 1988 to $95.3 billion.

Investors also show an increased awareness of the exchange privilege, which allows mutual fund shareholders to exchange shares from one fund to another within a group of funds under common management. This awareness, along with volatile financial markets, has encouraged investors to be flexible in the handling of their personal portfolios, producing a significant increase in exchange activity.

In 1988, for example, exchanges into all types of mutual funds totaled $134.3 billion, almost five times the level in the early part of the decade. As shown in the accompanying chart, total exchanges were only $28 billion in 1982. Since that date, exchanges have risen at a phenomenal rate. In general, exchange activity over the decade has concentrated in the shifting between long-term equity and bond funds and short-term money market funds as investors adjust their assets to correspond to their changing needs and to reflect their view of current market conditions.

In a relatively short period of time, mutual funds have become the nation's fourth largest type of financial institution. Only commercial banks, savings and loan institutions, and life insurance companies are larger in terms of assets.

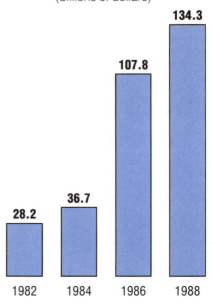

**Sales Exchanges
All Types of Mutual Funds**
(billions of dollars)

1982	1984	1986	1988
28.2	36.7	107.8	134.3

Responding to Investor Needs

One of the hallmarks of the mutual fund industry is its responsiveness in a rapidly changing economic environment. By keeping attuned to investor needs, the mutual fund industry has been able to adapt and expand its product line and services to suit just about any investor's goals.

As a result, the investor's choice of funds and investment objectives has grown dramatically. In 1975, mutual funds fit neatly into seven main categories. By the end of 1985, the seven fund categories had grown to 15, with many funds further defining their investment objectives according to industry sectors, geographic limitations, or business philosophies. The number of individual funds available almost quadrupled in that period. Continuing innovation in the variety of mutual fund portfolios being offered to the public further increased the investment objective categories in 1987 to 22.

With such a wide range of choices, the often-heard phrase, "Today, there's a mutual fund to meet every investor's needs!" is no exaggeration.

After providing the investing public with funds offering a full range of investment objectives, the industry's next priority has been ensuring prompt, professional service. In addition to the advantages their structure provides (as described on pages 7-10, "What Is a Mutual Fund?"), mutual funds offer a variety of other conveniences.

One such convenience is the ease of investing in a fund. Each fund establishes a minimum amount for opening an account plus minimum increments for adding to it. Some funds have very low minimums and others, none at all. Still others have minimums of $2,500 and up. The great majority fall between $250 and $1,000.

Funds try to make investing as easy as possible. Most have payroll deduction plans to take the effort out of making regular contributions.

Mutual funds also offer automatic reinvestment programs in which shareholders can elect to have dividends and capital gains distributions poured back into the fund by automatically buying new shares to expand their holdings.

A similar feature covers automatic withdrawal. Arrangements can be made with the fund to send checks from the fund's earnings or principal to the shareholder--or anyone else designated by the shareholder--also automatically.

Even if a shareholder is not participating in a regular withdrawal plan, the fund makes it easy to withdraw money. By law, the fund must be willing to redeem any or all shares on each business day. All a shareholder needs to do is give proper notification and the fund will send a check. Even easier is a shareholder's ability to write checks drawing from a money market mutual fund account and from some bond funds. While most funds have minimum check amounts of $500, this still proves a convenient way to redeem shares instantly.

If shareholders do not want to withdraw their money but, instead, want

Number of Mutual Funds
Classified by Investment Objective

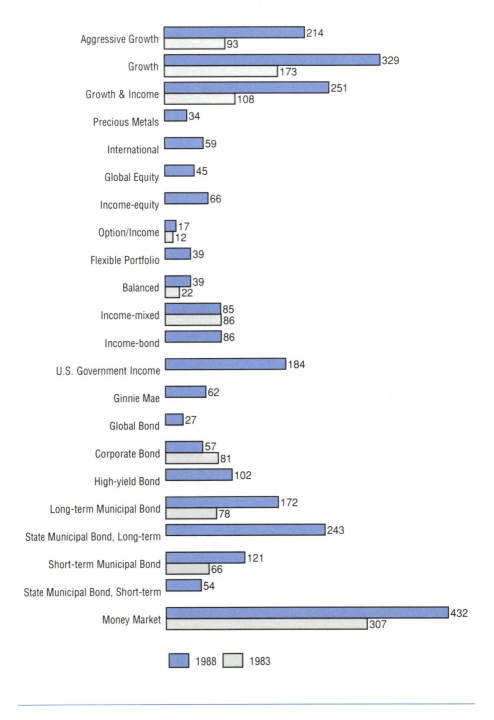

Investment Objective	1988	1983
Aggressive Growth	214	93
Growth	329	173
Growth & Income	251	108
Precious Metals	34	
International	59	
Global Equity	45	
Income-equity	66	
Option/Income	17	12
Flexible Portfolio	39	
Balanced	39	22
Income-mixed	85	86
Income-bond	86	
U.S. Government Income	184	
Ginnie Mae	62	
Global Bond	27	
Corporate Bond	57	81
High-yield Bond	102	
Long-term Municipal Bond	172	78
State Municipal Bond, Long-term	243	
Short-term Municipal Bond	121	66
State Municipal Bond, Short-term	54	
Money Market	432	307

■ 1988   □ 1983

to move their assets into a different fund, they can take advantage of a fund's exchange privilege. Many management companies offer more than one fund (known as a "family" of funds) to their shareholders. In this way, investors can choose from funds with a variety of investment objectives, each appropriate for different investor needs and economic conditions. An exchange privilege allows the shareholder to contact the fund or a fund representative at any time to exchange shares from one fund within the family to another. Usually funds allow investors to use the exchange privilege several times a year for a low or no fee per exchange.

Whenever a shareholder exchanges shares, writes a check from a money market fund, or makes an investment, a statement will be sent to confirm each transaction. Mutual funds have long been noted for their convenient recordkeeping. In addition to confirmation statements, the fund sends account updates on a monthly, quarterly, or annual basis, depending on the fund.

Finally, funds send periodic reports both to the SEC and to shareholders. Complete information is supplied to shareholders at least twice a year, and for most companies, four times a year. These reports list the names and the amount of securities the fund holds. They also show major investment changes since the last report, plus financial statements and related information.

The mutual fund industry tries to stay in tune with the needs of its current *and* future shareholders. Healthy competition ensures that the industry will continue to develop new products and services to respond to the needs of mutual fund shareholders better than ever.

Professional Management

Professional money management is one of the key features that draws investors to mutual funds. It is even more important today when many individuals find it increasingly difficult to make their own way in the securities markets.

The alternatives can seem endless and bewildering. Plus, many people do not have the time, inclination, or experience to choose and manage their own investments. Even individuals who *want* to make their own investment decisions sometimes feel squeezed out of the market by a phenomenon referred to as "the institutionalization of the market." Institutions are playing a much larger role in the securities markets through their big-volume trades executed by large "buy" and "sell" programs that can suddenly affect prices of securities. Takeover activity--and rumored activity--can also cause rapid fluctuations in securities prices. The average investor is finding it tougher and tougher to determine how market activity and fundamental economic changes affect individual securities and industries.

To invest more effectively today, millions of Americans have, in effect, hired professional money managers through mutual fund investing. No matter how modest their holdings, individual investors have joined the institutional investors by choosing mutual funds.

What Do the Money Managers Do?

Fund managers perform extensive economic and financial research. Their aim: to develop data so intelligent decisions can be made about securities in the fund's portfolio.

To make these decisions, investment analysts research basic economic trends--market conditions, interest rates, inflation--and then assess how individual companies and other security-issuing organizations will be affected. Managers read widely...not only general business publications, but also trade publications, research reports, and surveys. Their job means keeping up with the steady stream of financial information that companies release and file with various government agencies. They study balance sheets and other financial statements, companies' business systems and marketing philosophies, and talk to a cross-section of business executives. They may make field trips to inspect a company's plants. Often they specialize. One analyst may study utilities while a colleague concentrates on the computer industry. A third

Portfolio Composition of Equity, Bond, and Income Funds Yearend 1988
(billions of dollars)

Common Stock	$173.7
Preferred Stock	5.7
Municipal Bonds (long-term)	86.1
Corporate Bonds	54.4
U.S. Gov't Sec. (long-term)	103.8
U.S. Gov't Sec. (short-term)	11.1
Liquid Assets	34.0
Other	3.5
Total Net Assets	**$472.3**

may study stock markets overseas while another follows bonds or other debt issues.

Those responsible for managing the fund make buy and sell decisions for their portfolio, based on this research and the fund's investment objective. Typically, portfolio managers will invest the pool of shareholders' dollars in anywhere from 50 to over 100 different securities to diversify the fund's holdings.

Diversification

Diversification is a basic investment principle of all mutual funds. It means that the professional managers of mutual funds combine the money of shareholders and invest in many types of securities. It is a proven method of reducing the risk inherent in all investing.

Diversification may take different forms:

● Diversification among a variety of securities issuers--A number of federal and state regulations require this type of diversification. The Investment Company Act of 1940 sets minimum diver-

sification standards for a mutual fund to qualify as a diversified company; the Internal Revenue Code mandates a certain measure of diversification for a fund to qualify as a regulated investment company; and various states impose diversification requirements for a fund to be able to offer its shares in the state.

● Diversification among types of securities--Balanced funds are one example of this form of diversification. These funds invest in common stocks, preferred stocks, and corporate bonds.

● Diversification among a variety of industries--Stock funds diversify their portfolios by including securities issued by companies in many different industries. Corporate bond portfolios also include issues of different types of businesses, while those of municipal bond funds include holdings of a wide range of state and local governments.

● The exceptions--Not all funds are diversified across company, industry, and geographical lines. Specialty funds or sector funds focus on a specific industry, market segment, or geographic region. Examples include funds investing in high technology stocks, the health care industry, or sunbelt companies. But even in specialty funds, money managers still diversify within those specific areas.

Security Selection

The huge net sales volume of equity funds during the bull market years of the mid-'80s was a major source of liquidity in the securities market and helped to stimulate the financing of many new equity issues. Today, mutual fund managers must choose from thousands of different domestic securities issues with an estimated value of $3 trillion available on the organized exchanges and the over-the-counter markets in the U.S., plus thousands more in foreign issues traded on overseas exchanges. Mutual funds held $179 billion of those stocks in their portfolios in

Money Market Fund Asset Composition Yearend 1988
(billions of dollars)

U.S. Treasury Bills	$5.1
Other Treasury Securities	6.4
Other U.S. Securities	18.4
Repurchase Agreements	41.7
Commercial Bank CDs	26.6
Other Domestic CDs	6.1
Eurodollar CDs	29.7
Commercial Paper	117.1
Bankers Acceptances	12.0
Cash Reserves	0.7
Other	8.5
Total Net Assets	**$272.3**
Average Maturity (Days)	28
Number of Funds	432

Mutual Fund Investment Performance

Ten Years Through 12/31/88
(percentages)

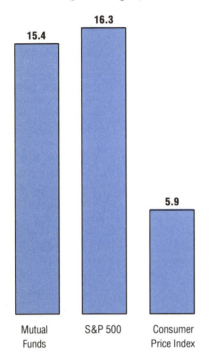

Mutual Funds	S&P 500	Consumer Price Index
15.4	16.3	5.9

Note: *Mutual fund performance reflects a monthly weighted average for all equity funds.*

Mutual fund and S&P 500 data are prepared by Lipper Analytical Services. These indexes are not adjusted for sales charges.

Money Market Mutual Funds Average Annual Yield

(percentages)

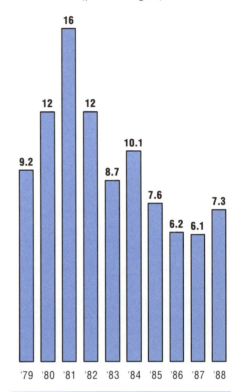

'79	'80	'81	'82	'83	'84	'85	'86	'87	'88
9.2	12	16	12	8.7	10.1	7.6	6.2	6.1	7.3

1988--representing thousands of different securities issues.

Funds purchase substantial amounts of corporate bonds and municipal securities, thereby helping finance corporate America as well as state and local governments. Mutual funds held $54 billion in corporate bonds and $86 billion in long-term municipal securities at the end of 1988.

In recent years, the mutual fund industry has also become an important market for government-backed mortgage securities (Ginnie Maes), Treasury bonds, and other government securities. Mutual funds currently hold about $115 billion worth of these securities in their portfolios.

Mutual funds, in short, do the job of an efficient financial intermediary. They gather up the public's savings and channel them into productive uses.

The tables at the end of this chapter represent the dollar value and market percentage for industries of special interest to equity fund managers in 1988. As might be expected, the ranking of various industries and the size of their share in fund portfolios change constantly. These variations reflect portfolio managers' evolving views of the attractiveness of securities from firms in different industry groups.

Dividends and Reinvestment
All Types of Mutual Funds
(billions of dollars)

Year	Investment Income Dividends	Reinvested Dividends	Percentage Reinvested
1975	$1.6	$1.1	68.1%
1976	1.7	1.1	63.1
1977	1.9	1.3	65.8
1978	2.5	1.8	71.3
1979	5.2	3.7	72.2
1980	10.4	8.5	81.3
1981	21.7	19.7	91.7
1982	25.8	22.9	88.8
1983	18.8	15.7	83.5
1984	23.7	18.4	77.6
1985	28.9	20.4	70.6
1986	35.8	25.5	71.2
1987	47.4	30.9	65.2
1988	53.4	33.2	62.2

Capital Gains and Dividends
Distributions to Shareholders
All Types of Mutual Funds
(billions of dollars)

Year	Net Realized Capital Gains	Net Investment Income Equity, Bond, and Income Funds	Money Market Funds	Short-term Municipal Bond Funds
1975	$0.2	$1.4	$0.2	NA
1976	0.5	1.6	0.1	NA
1977	0.6	1.8	0.1	NA
1978	0.7	2.1	0.4	NA
1979	0.9	2.5	2.7	NA
1980	1.7	2.7	7.7	$0.1
1981	2.7	3.1	18.5	0.1
1982	2.4	3.8	21.7	0.3
1983	4.4	5.0	13.2	0.6
1984	6.1	7.3	15.4	1.0
1985	5.0	12.9	14.4	1.6
1986	17.9	22.3	11.1	2.4
1987	23.0	31.8	12.8	2.8
1988	6.3	32.0	17.8	3.6

Diversification of Mutual Fund Portfolios
Common Stock Holdings by Industry
(millions of dollars)

	1987	1988
Agricultural Equipment	$710.8	$385.2
Aircraft Manufacturing & Aerospace	1,195.6	1,331.1
Air Transport	1,720.4	1,658.4
Auto & Accessories (excl. Tires)	3,853.7	3,525.4
Building Materials & Equipment	1,537.9	737.1
Chemicals	4,394.7	3,898.5
Communications (TV, Radio, Motion Pictures, Telephone)	5,618.2	6,194.5
Computer Services*	880.6	2,352.5
Conglomerates	2,003.0	1,973.9
Containers	632.2	115.4
Drugs & Cosmetics	4,587.7	3,778.2
Electric Equipment & Electronics (excl. TV & Radio)	8,047.0	3,538.0
Financial (incl. Banks & Insurance)	13,049.2	14,046.9
Foods and Beverages	2,146.6	2,431.3
Hospital Supplies & Services	1,107.4	1,062.9
Leisure Time	1,702.9	1,637.6
Machinery	1,487.1	1,424.0
Metals & Mining	3,221.9	2,440.0
Office Equipment	3,709.9	3,280.1
Oil	5,474.4	5,368.3
Paper	1,869.2	1,828.0
Printing & Publishing	1,295.0	1,240.1
Public Utilities (incl. Natural Gas)	5,097.3	4,605.8
Railroads & Railroad Equipment	1,435.6	962.5
Retail Trade	4,757.3	4,267.7
Rubber (incl. Tires)	623.0	275.7
Steel	443.4	459.5
Textiles	456.2	473.1
Tobacco	933.2	1,181.1
Trucking & Shipping	N/A	525.5
Miscellaneous	3,092.2	2,207.0
Total	**$87,088.6**	**$79,205.3**

Note: *Composite industry investments drawn from the portfolios of 60 of the largest investment companies as of the end of the calendar year 1988 whose total net assets represented 46.9% of total net assets of all reporting equity companies. Previous years not shown due to change in sample.*

Includes computer software, consultants, and time sharing.

Diversification of Mutual Fund Portfolios
Percent of Total Common Stock by Industry

	1987	1988
Agricultural Equipment	0.82%	0.49%
Aircraft Manufacturing & Aerospace	1.37	1.68
Air Transport	1.98	2.09
Auto & Accessories (excl. Tires)	4.42	4.45
Building Materials & Equipment	1.77	0.93
Chemicals	5.04	4.92
Communications (TV, Radio, Motion Pictures, Telephone)	6.45	7.82
Computer Services*	1.01	2.97
Conglomerates	2.30	2.49
Containers	0.73	0.15
Drugs & Cosmetics	5.27	4.77
Electric Equipment & Electronics (excl. TV & Radio)	9.24	4.47
Financial (incl. Banks & Insurance)	14.98	17.73
Foods and Beverages	2.46	3.07
Hospital Supplies & Services	1.27	1.34
Leisure Time	1.96	2.07
Machinery	1.71	1.8
Metals & Mining	3.70	3.08
Office Equipment	4.26	4.14
Oil	6.29	6.78
Paper	2.15	2.31
Printing & Publishing	1.49	1.57
Public Utilities (incl. Natural Gas)	5.85	5.81
Railroads & Railroad Equipment	1.65	1.21
Retail Trade	5.46	5.39
Rubber (incl. Tires)	0.72	0.35
Steel	0.51	0.58
Textiles	0.52	0.60
Tobacco	1.07	1.49
Trucking & Shipping	N/A	0.66
Miscellaneous	3.55	2.79
Total	**100.00%**	**100.00%**

Note: *Composite industry investments drawn from the portfolios of 60 of the largest investment companies as of the end of the calendar year 1988 whose total net assets represented 46.9% of total net assets of all reporting equity companies. Previous years not shown due to change in sample.*

*Includes computer software, consultants, and time sharing.

Recent Trends in Activity:
Stock, Bond, and Income Funds

Despite a year of moderate economic growth and increases in stock and bond prices, investor uncertainty with regard to the financial markets was still a factor one year after the 1987 market break. At yearend 1988, total sales of stock, bond, and income funds reached only about half the level of 1987 total sales-- $95.3 billion in 1988 compared to $190.6 billion in 1987.

The sales of each broad type of fund diminished: stock fund sales in 1988 were $31 billion, down from $72.1 billion in 1987, and bond and income fund sales were $64.3 billion in 1988, compared to $118.6 billion in 1987. Nevertheless, sales of long-term funds are still impressive when measured against historical levels; at yearend 1988, they reached their fourth highest level ever.

Share of Equity Funds
Sales and Redemptions Annually

	Sales		Redemptions	
	1987	1988	1987	1988
Aggressive Growth	16.3%	14.1%	17.9%	15.0%
Growth	24.6	27.0	27.2	28.4
Growth & Income	32.4	34.0	27.3	31.5
Precious Metals	4.4	3.8	4.6	3.5
International	5.8	3.9	7.6	5.2
Global Equity	4.3	4.4	5.0	5.3
Income-equity	9.4	10.0	6.8	6.8
Option/Income	2.8	2.8	3.6	4.3
Total	**100.0%**	**100.0%**	**100.0%**	**100.0%**

Share of Bond and Income Funds
Sales and Redemptions Annually

	Sales		Redemptions	
	1987	1988	1987	1988
Flexible Portfolio	2.5%	1.7%	0.7%	1.8%
Balanced	2.8	2.0	1.5	2.9
Income-mixed	5.0	4.2	6.3	5.9
Income-bond	4.5	5.7	4.2	4.7
U.S. Government Income	37.1	25.9	36.0	36.2
Ginnie Mae	11.2	7.1	17.1	12.4
Global Bond	0.9	2.3	0.6	1.3
Corporate Bond	3.1	3.6	2.9	3.3
High-yield Bond	8.5	15.3	7.8	9.6
Long-term Municipal Bond	15.2	19.6	15.4	14.5
State Municipal Bond, Long-term	9.2	12.6	7.5	7.4
Total	**100.0%**	**100.0%**	**100.0%**	**100.0%**

Mutual Fund Assets
Classified by Investment Objective
Yearend (billions of dollars)

Investment Objective	1987	1988	Percent Change
Aggressive Growth	$27.3	$29.5	+8.1%
Growth	48.0	50.5	+5.2
Growth & Income	64.0	70.9	+10.8
Precious Metals	4.1	3.2	-22.0
International	7.0	6.8	-2.9
Global Equity	10.4	11.1	+6.7
Income-equity	14.7	17.5	+19.0
Option/Income	5.1	5.3	+3.9
Flexible Portfolio	4.3	3.5	-18.6
Balanced	9.0	9.5	+5.6
Income-mixed	11.4	8.8	-22.8
Income-bond	12.6	10.7	-15.1
U.S. Government Income	88.9	82.7	-7.0
Ginnie Mae	34.2	28.7	-16.1
Global Bond	2.1	3.0	+42.9
Corporate Bond	9.5	10.5	+10.5
High-yield Bond	24.2	33.4	+38.0
Long-term Municipal Bond	49.2	54.3	+10.4
State Municipal Bond, Long-term	27.8	32.4	+16.5
*Total Long-term Funds	$453.8	$472.3	+4.1%

*See next chapter for total short-term fund (money market and short-term municipal bond funds) assets.

Mutual Fund Sales
Classified by Investment Objective
(millions of dollars)

Investment Objective	1987	1988	Percent Change
Aggressive Growth	$11,756.1	$4,361.4	-62.9%
Growth	17,723.5	8,386.3	-52.7
Growth & Income	23,320.1	10,555.6	-54.7
Precious Metals	3,180.8	1,193.3	-62.5
International	4,183.6	1,214.4	-71.0
Global Equity	3,130.4	1,348.4	-56.9
Income-equity	6,760.2	3,088.3	-54.3
Option/Income	2,011.1	866.5	-56.9
Flexible Portfolio	2,966.3	1,075.8	-63.7
Balanced	3,263.4	1,291.0	-60.4
Income-mixed	5,915.5	2,714.3	-54.1
Income-bond	5,400.6	3,634.1	-32.7
U.S. Government Income	44,033.0	16,636.3	-66.2
Ginnie Mae	13,251.1	4,548.8	-65.7
Global Bond	1,118.7	1,509.0	34.9
Corporate Bond	3,683.5	2,289.5	-37.8
High-yield Bond	10,020.1	9,828.2	-1.9
Long-term Municipal Bond	17,991.1	12,626.2	-29.8
State Municipal Bond, Long-term	10,918.9	8,125.5	-25.6
*Total Long-term Funds	$190,628.0	$95,292.9	-50.0%

*See next chapter for total short-term fund (money market and short-term municipal bond funds) assets.

The leading stock fund category in 1988 was growth and income funds with $10.5 billion in sales, followed by growth funds with $8.3 billion, and aggressive growth funds with $4.3 billion.

Bond and income funds continued the trend of recent years and outsold stock funds by a wide margin. The 1988 figure of $64.3 billion in bond and income fund sales represents twice the sales volume of equity fund sales in 1988. Compared with the previous year, though, the sales of all categories of bond and income funds declined, with one exception: global bond funds increased from $1.1 billion in sales in 1987 to $1.5 billion in 1988. High-yield bond funds most nearly maintained the sales level of the previous year and totaled

$9.8 billion in 1988 compared to $10.0 billion in 1987.

The overall drop in sales of long-term mutual funds in 1988 can be attributed to two main causes: the investment uncertainty created by the 1987 stock market break, particularly in the first part of the year, and to the surge in short-term interest rates, which stimulated investors' appetite for money market and other short-term mutual funds.

Clearly, 1988 saw the introduction of a substantially different market environment. Moving swiftly to meet the new challenges, the mutual fund industry repeated a historical pattern of responding to, and frequently anticipating, investor needs with new types of investment products and services. For example, five years ago, falling

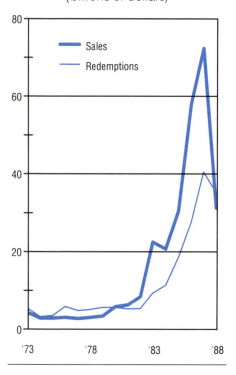

Sales and Redemptions Equity Funds

(billions of dollars)

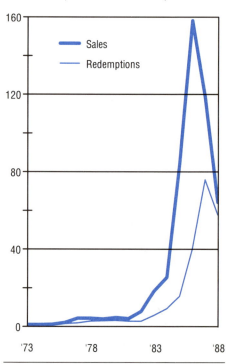

Sales and Redemptions Bond and Income Funds

(billions of dollars)

Assets of Equity and Bond & Income Funds

(billions of dollars)

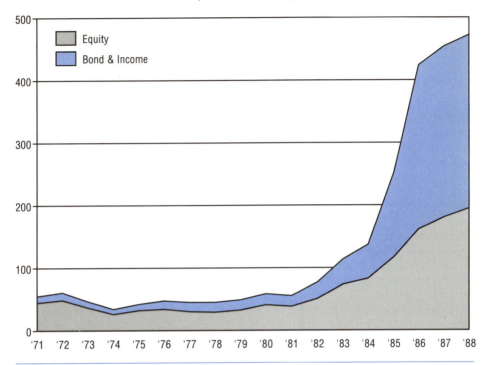

Equity
Bond & Income

interest rates propelled many investors into the newer, more income-oriented funds such as government and GNMA funds. Here, they obtained attractive real rates of return by assuming moderate levels of risk relative to some other investment options. But as the economic climate changed, investors turned to other types of funds, including a variety of stock funds, to take advantage of a vigorous bull market. In 1988, a steady pace of new funds was introduced to the mar-

ket, many of which were designed to meet investors' desire for safety of principal.

Recent asset figures attest to the effectiveness of the industry's product development efforts. Total long-term fund assets increased in 1988 to close the year at new heights--$810.3 billion. In comparison, assets at the end of 1987 were $769.9 billion, and $716.2 billion at yearend 1986. Assets at the beginning of the decade were only $94.5 billion.

Recent Trends in Activity:
Money Market and Short-term Municipal Bond Funds

Despite the changed economic climate of 1988, total assets of money market funds (MMFs) ended the year at the historic high of $272.3 billion, a 6.9 percent increase from the 1987 yearend total of $254.7 billion. In 1988, money market funds benefited from both a widespread migration of investors to safer investments and a jump in short-term yields. Money market fund yields rose to an average of 7.3 percent in 1988, the highest average yield since 1985 (see chart, p. 24).

Money market fund assets increased steadily over the past five years, a far cry from the roller coaster ride these assets had taken previously. From the 1982 figure of $206.6 billion, money market fund assets plummeted over $44.1 billion a year later to $162.5 billion at the end of 1983, owing to the competition from banks' newly authorized money market deposit accounts (MMDAs) and rising stock and bond prices. But then the situation leveled off. Since August 1983, MMF rates have consistently been higher than those of MMDAs, and 1984 saw the industry recoup much of its losses, ending that year at $209.7 billion.

In addition to the attractiveness of money market funds because of increased demand for conservative financial products and higher yields, the appeal of MMFs lies in their versatility.

There are three main ways people use money market funds. These vary in importance, depending on market conditions. One major way to use a money market fund is as a cash management tool--a way to earn market rates on money to be used for paying the common bills of everyday life. (Institutions use money market funds this way on a larger scale.) Another is as a savings instrument. And third, money market funds are used as a safe harbor between financial transactions.

Investors have come to recognize the importance of money market funds in every financial plan. For that reason, there will probably be a relatively stable, ongoing use of these funds as cash management tools. The amount of money people keep in these funds may fluctuate with the changing forces in the market, but money market funds will continue to play a role in responding to investors' needs for a relatively safe, high-yielding, liquid instrument.

There are three broad types of money market funds offering shares--each responding to somewhat different needs. General purpose funds and broker/dealer funds, for example, both sell to individuals and to institutions. Individuals, however, are the primary market and represent over 70 percent of the assets of both types of funds. Conversely, institutional funds concentrate primarily on institutional investors such as businesses and bank trust departments. These funds are characterized by fewer shareholders with larger amounts to invest.

At the end of 1988, of the $272.3 billion in assets, $114.7 billion or 42 percent was in broker/dealer funds.

Weekly Yield on MMFs and MMDAs
January 1, 1987 - December 31, 1988

(percentages)

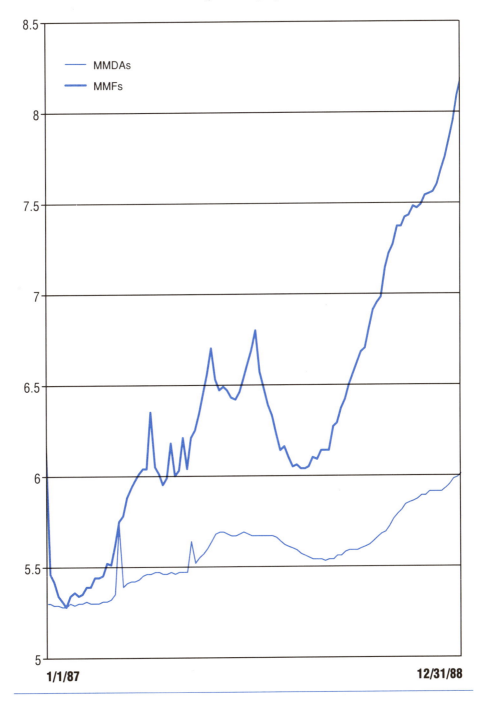

Money Market Fund Assets and Shareholder Accounts

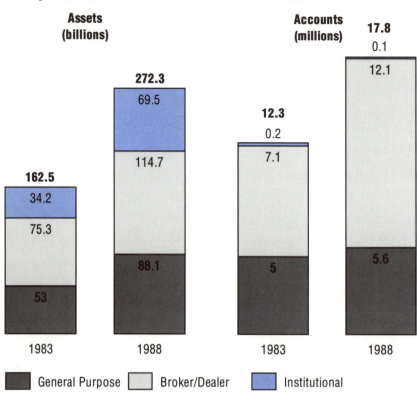

Assets (billions)

162.5	
34.2	
75.3	
53	
1983	

272.3	
69.5	
114.7	
88.1	
1988	

Accounts (millions)

12.3	
0.2	
7.1	
5	
1983	

17.8	
0.1	
12.1	
5.6	
1988	

■ General Purpose   □ Broker/Dealer   ■ Institutional

Short-term Municipal Bond Fund Assets and Shareholder Accounts

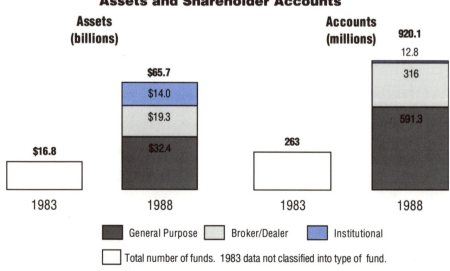

Assets (billions)

$16.8 — 1983

$65.7 — 1988
$14.0
$19.3
$32.4

Accounts (millions)

263 — 1983

920.1 — 1988
12.8
316
591.3

■ General Purpose   □ Broker/Dealer   ■ Institutional

□ Total number of funds. 1983 data not classified into type of fund.

General purpose funds had $88.1 billion and institutional funds held $69.5 billion, 32 percent and 26 percent respectively.

Shareholder accounts in money market funds have risen in 1988 to a new record level of 17.8 million. Again, the broker/dealer funds held the largest portion of accounts, making up 68 percent of the market, while general purpose funds accounted for 31 percent. As noted earlier, institutional funds have fewer accounts with large account balances. These funds represent less than 1 percent of all money market fund accounts.

While the money market funds were growing at a healthy rate in 1988, their tax-exempt counterparts, short-term municipal bond funds, were also growing. These funds, introduced in 1979 with assets of $0.3 billion, ended 1988 with $65.7 billion in assets. At the end of 1987 they had

assets of $61.4 billion, although 1987 assets had reached as high as $70.2 billion during the year. Part of the appeal of these funds (sometimes referred to as tax-exempt money market funds) is the combination of standard money market fund features with the bonus of tax-free income. While the lower income tax rates imposed by the Tax Reform Act of 1986 undoubtedly diminished some investor interest, short-term municipal bond funds remained particularly attractive to investors subject to the top marginal tax rate of 33 percent.

The continued growth in accounts of short-term municipal bond funds demonstrates the appeal they have for investors. Total accounts rose in 1988 to 920,089, compared with 842,124 in 1987, indicating that they are a significant product in the diverse mutual fund marketplace.

How Mutual Fund Shares Are Acquired by Investors

Many kinds of firms provide a wide range of products and services in today's securities industry. Some offer investment advice, financial planning, insurance, and commodity products, in addition to such traditional services as executing orders to buy and sell securities and underwriting new stock and bond issues. Some firms offer a few of these products and services, while others only execute trades for investors who have made their own investment decisions.

Considering the securities industry's complexity, it is not surprising that mutual funds' distribution patterns have become equally diverse. Some funds offer their shares to investors through the mail, by telephone, or at their own offices while others sell through securities firms, financial planners, life insurance organizations, other financial institutions, or even through membership organizations.

Basically, however, mutual fund distribution can be broken down into two major channels: shares purchased from a member of a sales force and shares purchased directly from a fund. These two distribution channels are frequently referred to as "sales force" and "direct marketing," respectively.

Most mutual funds are affiliated with an underwriter that distributes their shares nationally. The underwriter has exclusive distribution rights and may use several different avenues for share distribution.

The Broker/Dealer: Most often, the underwriter distributes fund shares through securities firms and their brokers. These brokers deal directly with the public--the potential purchasers of mutual fund shares.

In addition to traditional broker/dealer firms, an increasing number of financial planners are recommending mutual funds to their clients. More and more, financial planners suggest mutual funds as building blocks in a master financial plan, which might also include life insurance and individual securities.

Within the broker/dealer distribution system, underwriters, in effect, act as wholesalers. Underwriters do not sell shares to the public directly. Instead, they establish sales agreements with securities firms which, in turn, sell the fund's shares to individual investors through the firms' branch offices. To assist local firms and branches, a mutual fund underwriter usually divides the country into regions and assigns its own staff members to represent the underwriter in each area.

Retail securities firms distributing mutual fund shares are usually members of the National Association of Securities Dealers, Inc. (NASD). This organization provides self-policing of its member firms in the distribution of mutual fund shares, as well as in over-the-counter securities transactions.

Captive (or Dedicated) Sales Force: In some cases, an underwriter employs its own sales force. These

Sales of Sales Force & Direct Marketing Funds by Investment Objective - 1988

(percentages)

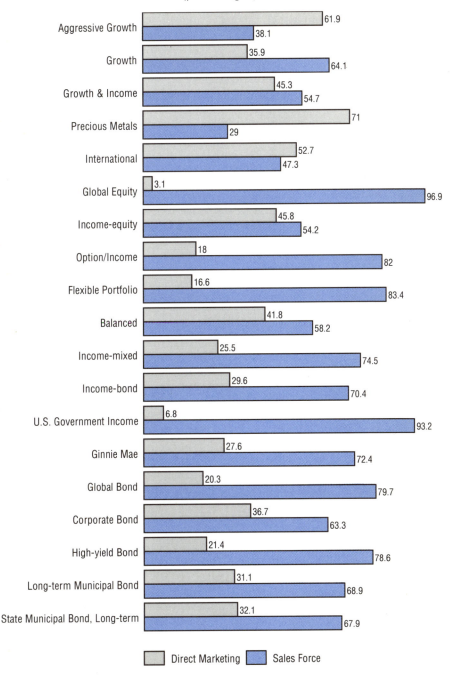

Investment Objective	Direct Marketing	Sales Force
Aggressive Growth	61.9	38.1
Growth	35.9	64.1
Growth & Income	45.3	54.7
Precious Metals	71	29
International	52.7	47.3
Global Equity	3.1	96.9
Income-equity	45.8	54.2
Option/Income	18	82
Flexible Portfolio	16.6	83.4
Balanced	41.8	58.2
Income-mixed	25.5	74.5
Income-bond	29.6	70.4
U.S. Government Income	6.8	93.2
Ginnie Mae	27.6	72.4
Global Bond	20.3	79.7
Corporate Bond	36.7	63.3
High-yield Bond	21.4	78.6
Long-term Municipal Bond	31.1	68.9
State Municipal Bond, Long-term	32.1	67.9

Direct Marketing ▢   Sales Force ▢

people primarily sell shares of the funds the underwriter represents plus other securities issued by the underwriter and its affiliates. In some cases, a captive sales force is the sales arm of an insurance company which might own a mutual fund management company.

Fund shares sold through brokers, commission-based financial planners, or dedicated sales forces may have a sales charge included in their offering price. Depending on the type of fund, the charge (usually referred to as a "load") may range from 4 to 8.5 percent. Usually, the basic charge will vary, depending on the size of the purchase. In addition, some funds assign a small percentage of fund assets to aid in distribution expenses. These charges, referred to as 12b-1 fees, may range up to about 1.25 percent per year. Usually 12b-1 funds sold by a broker or planner have no up-front sales charge or load. But there may be a declining charge if shares are redeemed during the first few years of ownership. These charges are often called contingent-deferred sales charges or "back-end loads."

Mutual funds are required to redeem outstanding shares at their current net asset value each day. This is the case regardless of distribution method or commission structure.

Fund to Investor: In this method of distribution, investors purchase mutual fund shares directly from the fund--usually by mail, telephone, bank wire, or sometimes at offices maintained by fund organizations. As a technical matter, however, these direct marketing funds usually have an underwriter--a distribution arm of the fund organization--through which all share transactions pass.

The funds attract investors through advertising, direct mail, and other means. Potential investors do their own research and take the initiative to determine if specific funds meet their needs. Investors contact the fund organization directly to obtain a prospectus or buy shares. The shares of these funds are generally sold to the public with a low sales charge or none at all. The latter are usually referred to as "no-load."

Sales by Method of Distribution

Of all stock, bond, and income fund sales made in the mutual fund industry in 1988, $65.0 billion or 68 percent were made by those funds distributed through a sales force. Those funds distributed directly to investors had sales of $27.2 billion or 29 percent of the total. (Other sales resulted from reinvested dividends in funds no longer offering shares and from variable annuities.)

Among equity funds, the two major methods of distribution--through a sales force or direct marketing--recorded sales of $16.3 billion and $12.8 billion, respectively. The sales force distribution channels attained their highest percentage of overall sales through $48.7 billion in bond and income fund sales. Direct marketing sales were $14.4 billion in the bond and income funds.

Where the Most Funds Are Purchased

Assets and sales of mutual funds are heaviest in geographic regions with large numbers of people in moderate- to upper-income groups. As may be seen in the accompanying chart, California and New York accounted for the two largest state shares of total sales of equity, bond, and income funds. Sales in California totaled $13.5 billion in 1988, 14.6 percent of all sales of those funds. New York fund sales totaled $11.0 billion, 11.9 percent of total sales. The ten states with the largest share of stock and bond fund sales, moreover, accounted for over 63.4 percent of the total.

Equity, Bond, and Income Fund Sales by Selected States - 1988

(billions of dollars)

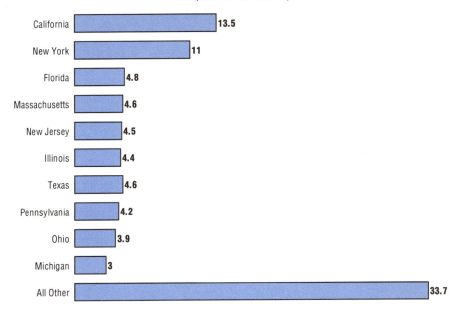

California	13.5
New York	11
Florida	4.8
Massachusetts	4.6
New Jersey	4.5
Illinois	4.4
Texas	4.6
Pennsylvania	4.2
Ohio	3.9
Michigan	3
All Other	33.7

The Retirement Market

Mutual funds are especially compatible with the long-term objectives of saving for retirement because:

• There is a fund to match any long-term objective and risk/reward preference.

• Families of funds provide great flexibility through the exchange feature, enabling shareholders to adjust their holdings to economic conditions as well as to changes in their personal financial circumstances.

• Mutual funds work best over long periods of time, when allowed to ride out the ups and downs of market cycles.

• Funds provide a wide range of services, such as automatic withdrawal plans and complete recordkeeping. (See box on page 44 for descriptions of various retirement plans.)

IRAs

The Individual Retirement Account (IRA) market has rapidly grown to command the largest share of the mutual fund industry's retirement assets.

Although the Tax Reform Act of 1986 modified the ground rules for IRAs,

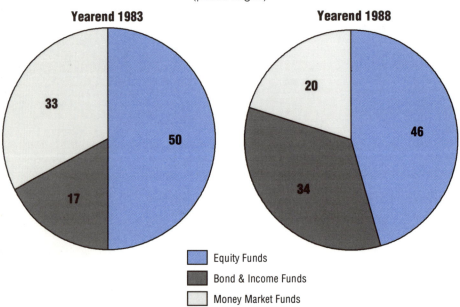

IRA Assets by Type of Fund
(percentages)

Yearend 1983

33
50
17

Yearend 1988

20
46
34

- Equity Funds
- Bond & Income Funds
- Money Market Funds

they are still a strong mutual fund market.

In 1981, before IRAs were liberalized to allow all working Americans to create do-it-yourself retirement programs, mutual funds had only $2.6 billion of assets in 500,000 IRA accounts. By the end of 1988, mutual fund IRA assets had climbed to $86.0 billion in 15.7 million accounts. Compared to 1987, mutual fund IRA assets increased by $13.7 billion and the number of accounts increased by almost 700,000. Of the industry's $86.0 billion in IRA assets, $39.2 billion or 45.6 percent of assets were in equity funds, $29.4 billion or 34.2 percent of assets were in bond and income funds, and $17.4 billion or 20.2 percent were in money market funds.

Of the 15.7 million IRA accounts, equity funds had 7.8 million, bond and income funds had 3.8 million, and money market funds had 4.1 million. At the end of 1981, when IRAs were liberalized, only 1 percent of all mutual fund assets were held in IRA accounts. At the end of 1988, that share had grown to 10.6 percent.

In addition, 28.5 percent of all mutual fund accounts are IRA accounts. (Some IRA mutual fund shareholders hold multiple accounts.)

At the end of 1981, when all Americans with earned income became eligible for IRAs, mutual funds accounted for 9.9 percent of all IRA assets in the marketplace. Growth in mutual fund IRA assets since that time occurred at a greater rate than growth in competing investments, resulting in an increased share of the IRA market for mutual funds. Mutual funds in 1988 accounted for about 22 percent of the total IRA market.

The Tax Reform Act of 1986 brought significant changes to IRAs (see boxed section in this chapter on page 44). Nevertheless, about 87 percent of American households are still able to take a full or partial IRA deduction. For instance, any individual who is not covered by an employer-provided pension plan, and whose spouse is not covered by an employer-provided pension plan, can take the full IRA deduction without regard to the amount of earned income. Furthermore, the tax deferral that IRAs provide is a powerful wealth-building tool. Other positive factors that will

Estimated Value of IRA Plans
(value in billions of dollars/percent market share)

	12/84		12/86		12/88	
Commercial Banks	$37.2	28.2%	$67.0	24.2%	$88.0	22.4%
Thrifts	43.4	32.9	69.0	24.9	90.0	22.9
Life Insurance Companies	12.6	9.5	22.0	7.9	36.0	9.1
Credit Unions	7.8	5.9	20.5	7.4	25.0	6.4
Mutual Funds	16.5	12.5	53.7	19.4	86.0	21.9
Self-directed	14.6	11.0	44.9	16.2	68.0	17.3
Total IRA Dollar Value	**$132.1**	**100.0%**	**$277.1**	**100.0%**	**$393.0**	**100.0%**

affect the mutual fund IRA market in the future include the large number of outstanding IRA accounts held elsewhere whose owners may turn to mutual funds for improved performance, the benefit of professional money management, and the convenience of recordkeeping that funds offer IRA shareholders. Thus, IRAs should continue to be an important market for mutual funds in the post tax-reform environment.

Retirement Plans for the Self-employed

Mutual funds, traditionally holding close to a third of the market for retirement plans for the self-employed (also known as Keogh plans), had more than 810,000 of these accounts under management at the end of 1988. These plans totaled $10.8 billion in assets.

As may be seen in the accompanying chart, 47.3 percent of these retirement plans' assets managed by mutual funds were in equity funds, money market funds accounted for 30.7 percent, and bond and income funds had 22.0 percent of assets.

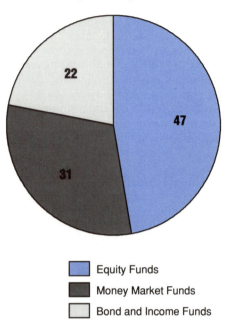

Self-employed Retirement Plan Assets by Type of Fund Yearend 1988

(percentages)

47
31
22

■ Equity Funds
■ Money Market Funds
□ Bond and Income Funds

Mutual Fund IRAs by Investment Objective

Investment Objective	Percent of Assets as of 12/31/88
Aggressive Growth	10.0%
Growth	10.3
Growth & Income	14.3
Precious Metals	0.9
International	1.4
Global Equity	2.9
Income-equity	4.9
Option/Income	1.0
Flexible Portfolio	1.0
Balanced	1.7
Income-mixed	1.5
Income-bond	1.7
U.S. Government Income	13.6
Ginnie Mae	5.0
Global Bond	0.2
Corporate Bond	2.2
High-yield Bond	7.2
Money Market	20.2

Growth in Mutual Fund IRA Plans - 1988

Accounts (millions)

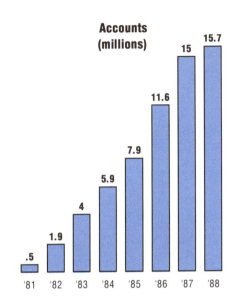

'81	'82	'83	'84	'85	'86	'87	'88
.5	1.9	4	5.9	7.9	11.6	15	15.7

Assets (billions)

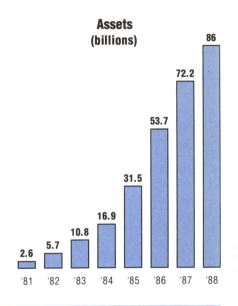

'81	'82	'83	'84	'85	'86	'87	'88
2.6	5.7	10.8	16.9	31.5	53.7	72.2	86

Growth in Mutual Fund Self-employed Retirement Plans - 1988

Accounts (thousands)

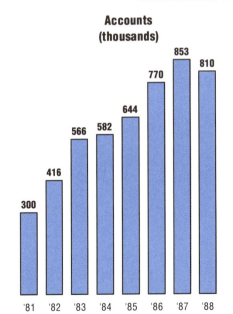

'81	'82	'83	'84	'85	'86	'87	'88
300	416	566	582	644	770	853	810

Assets (billions)

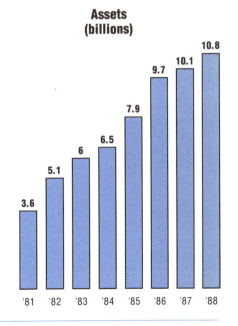

'81	'82	'83	'84	'85	'86	'87	'88
3.6	5.1	6	6.5	7.9	9.7	10.1	10.8

Retirement Plans

Federal income tax laws permit the establishment of a number of types of retirement plans, each of which may be funded with mutual fund shares.

Individual Retirement Accounts

All wage-earners under the age of 70½ may set up an Individual Retirement Account (IRA). The individual may contribute as much as 100 percent of his or her compensation each year, up to $2,000. Earnings are tax-deferred until withdrawal. The amount contributed each year may be wholly or partially tax-deductible. Under the Tax Reform Act of 1986, all taxpayers not covered by employer-sponsored retirement plans can continue to take the full deduction for IRA contributions. Those who are covered, or who are married to someone who is covered, must have an adjusted gross income of no more than $25,000 (single) or $40,000 (married, filing jointly) to take the full deduction. The deduction is phased out for incomes between $25,000 and $35,000 (single) and $40,000 and $50,000 (married, filing jointly). An individual who qualifies for an IRA and has a spouse who either has no earnings or elects to be treated as having no earnings, may contribute up to 100 percent of his or her income or $2,250, whichever is less.

Simplified Employee Pensions (SEPs)

SEPs are employer-sponsored plans that may be viewed as an aggregation of separate IRAs. In a SEP, the employer contributes up to $30,000 or 15 percent of compensation, whichever is less, to an Individual Retirement Account maintained for the employee.

Section 403(b) Plans

Section 403(b) of the Internal Revenue Code permits employees of certain charitable organizations and public school systems to establish tax-sheltered retirement programs. These plans may be invested in either annuity contracts or mutual fund shares.

Section 401(k) Plans

One particularly popular type of plan which may be offered by either corporate or non-corporate entities is the 401(k) plan. A 401(k) plan is a tax-qualified profit-sharing plan that includes a "cash or deferred" arrangement. The cash or deferred arrangement permits employees to have a portion of their compensation contributed to a tax-sheltered plan on their behalf or paid to them directly as additional taxable compensation. Thus an employee may elect to reduce his or her taxable compensation with contributions to a 401(k) plan where those amounts will accumulate tax-free. The Tax Reform Act of 1986 established new, tighter antidiscrimination requirements for 401(k) plans and curtailed the amount of elective deferrals which may be made by all employees. Nevertheless, 401(k) plans remain excellent and popular retirement savings vehicles.

Corporate and Self-employed Retirement Plans

Tax-qualified pension and profit-sharing plans may be established by corporations or self-employed individuals. Changes in the tax laws have made retirement plans for employees of corporations and those for self-employed individuals essentially comparable. Contributions to a plan are tax-deductible and earnings accumulate on a tax-sheltered basis.

The maximum annual amount which may be contributed to a defined contribution plan on behalf of an individual is limited to the lesser of 25 percent of the individual's compensation or $30,000.

Comparative Equity Performance Annualized Ten-year Total Return

(Period Ending December 31, 1988)
(percentages)

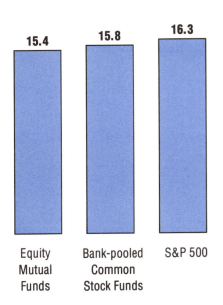

15.4 — Equity Mutual Funds
15.8 — Bank-pooled Common Stock Funds
16.3 — S&P 500

Source: ICI monthly asset weighted average equity fund performance and the S&P 500 returns are compiled by Lipper Analytical Services. The bank-pooled common stock fund asset weighted returns from data are compiled by CDA, Inc.

Total Net Assets Held in Pension and Profit-sharing Accounts in Mutual Funds Yearend 1988

(billions of dollars)

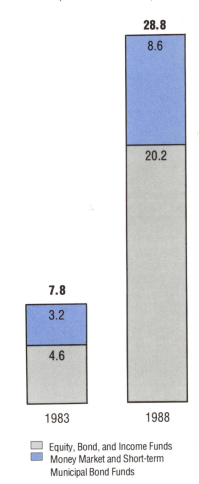

1983: 7.8 (3.2 / 4.6)
1988: 28.8 (8.6 / 20.2)

☐ Equity, Bond, and Income Funds
☐ Money Market and Short-term Municipal Bond Funds

The self-employed retirement plan market has become increasingly important since the liberalization of the tax laws in 1982. This change eliminated most of the distinctions between corporate plans and plans maintained for the self-employed, and allowed self-employed individuals to put away the lesser of 25 percent of income or $30,000.

Although the law no longer distinguishes between plans for the self-employed and corporate pension plans, many new restrictions apply to any plan which is a "top-heavy" plan, i.e., a plan under which a substantial portion of the benefits accrue on behalf of certain key employees of the employer. Many Keogh plans are treated as top-heavy plans subject to the aforementioned restrictions. Many mutual fund complexes offer prototype top-heavy plans that comply with all of the new provisions of law.

Corporate Plans

In recent years, mutual funds have made substantial progress in attracting corporate pension and profit-sharing accounts. Corporate plan sponsors have come to appreciate the built-in advantages mutual funds can offer their plans. Mutual funds give them access to top professional money managers, instant diversification, a portfolio managed according to a well-defined philosophy and policy, liquidity, and ease of administration.

Institutional Markets

Perhaps more than most other investments, mutual funds are especially important to small investors. The modest initial investment requirements, plus investors' ability to add relatively small amounts to their accounts at regular intervals, help explain why mutual funds are so popular to this group. Outstanding investment performance, diversification, and other services available through mutual funds, however, also attract fund investors in middle- and upper-income brackets. But these groups are not alone in their enthusiastic embrace of mutual funds. Increasingly, institutions are turning to mutual funds as an investment option.

Banks and other fiduciaries, business corporations, employee pension and profit-sharing plans, insurance companies, and foundations are among the institutions utilizing mutual funds. As the accompanying chart shows, the value of institutional assets under management has risen from about $6.2 billion in 1970 to $262.0 billion at the end of 1988.

Since this rate of growth has been much more rapid than the expansion of assets owned by individuals, institutional assets have accounted for an expanding share of total mutual fund assets. Between the end of 1960 and the end of 1988, the share of total assets accounted for by institutions rose from 10.6 percent to 32.3 percent. Part of the reason for the acceleration in institutional activity has been the expansion of money market funds, which were first offered in the mid-1970s.

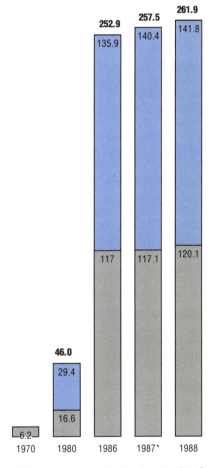

Total Institutional Assets in Mutual Funds
(billions of dollars)

| Money Market and Short-term Municipal Bond Funds |
| Equity, Bond and Income Funds |

* Revised

Institutional Assets by Type of Institution - 1988
(billions of dollars)

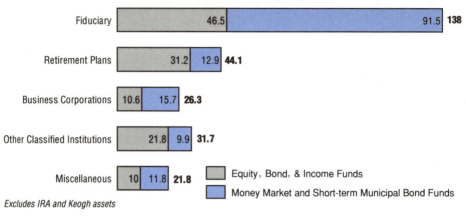

	Equity, Bond, & Income Funds
Fiduciary	46.5	91.5	**138**
Retirement Plans	31.2	12.9	**44.1**
Business Corporations	10.6	15.7	**26.3**
Other Classified Institutions	21.8	9.9	**31.7**
Miscellaneous	10	11.8	**21.8**

☐ Equity, Bond, & Income Funds
☐ Money Market and Short-term Municipal Bond Funds

Excludes IRA and Keogh assets

Institutional assets represented 43.0 percent of total money market fund assets at the end of 1988. Reflecting the overall changed economic climate in 1988 and its effect on asset levels in general, institutional assets in money market funds rose modestly in 1988 to $117.0 billion from $114.3 billion in 1987.

Similarly, institutional assets in stock, bond, and income funds were marginally higher in 1988 with $120.1 billion, up from $117.1 billion at year-end 1987. Total assets of these funds increased at a greater rate, which resulted in a small decline in the share of assets held by institutions. At the end of 1988, 25.4 percent of total assets were held by institutions, down very slightly from the 25.8 percent share they represented at the end of 1987.

The number of institutional accounts has expanded over the years, along with the rise in assets. In 1960, there were only about 347,000 accounts on the books. At the end of 1988, institutional accounts totaled 6.3 million. Since many of these are pooled accounts, the number of fund customers linked to institutions is even larger.

The institutional market is complex and includes a number of sub-markets, each of which has many unique characteristics. By far, the largest such market is the fiduciary group, which has over 50 percent of all institutional assets and accounts.

At the end of 1988, fiduciary accounts of all types of funds numbered about 3.2 million and had an estimated total value of $138.0 billion.

The fiduciary market is composed of at least two broad segments: bank trusts and individuals serving as trustees, guardians, and administrators. The former market is served mainly by the money market funds, while the latter is primarily the province of all other types of funds. This distinction is evident from the fact that the average-size fiduciary account associated with money market funds is much larger than stock, bond, and income funds.

Other statistical details relating to the institutional market are contained in tables presented in the data section of the Fact Book.

Regulation and Taxation

Mutual fund organizations are perhaps the most strictly regulated business entities under the federal securities laws. A former chairman of the SEC said, "No issuer of securities is subject to more detailed regulation than mutual funds."

The laws governing mutual funds require exhaustive disclosure to the SEC, state regulators, and fund shareholders and entail continuous regulation of fund operations. Appropriately, however, these laws do not include second-guessing of the investment judgment of each fund's management (provided the fund is invested according to the objectives and any restrictions set forth in its prospectus and according to federal and state law).

Four major federal statutes regulate mutual funds.

The Securities Act of 1933 requires filing with the SEC a registration statement that contains extensive information regarding the fund. In addition, the 1933 act requires the fund to provide potential investors with a current prospectus. The prospectus contains detailed disclosures about the fund's management, its investment policies, objectives, and other essential data. The 1933 act also limits the type and content of advertisements that may be used by a mutual fund.

The purchase and sale of mutual fund shares, as with all securities, are subject to the antifraud provisions of the Securities Exchange Act of 1934. Distributors of mutual fund shares are subject to regulation by the SEC and the NASD pursuant to the 1934 act.

The Investment Advisers Act of 1940 regulates the activities of investment advisers to mutual funds.

Most important, the mutual fund must register with the SEC under the Investment Company Act of 1940, which is a highly detailed regulatory statute. The 1940 act contains numerous provisions designed to prevent self-dealing and other conflicts of interest, maintain the integrity of fund assets, and prevent the fund and its shareholders from paying excessive fees and charges.

In addition to these federal statutes, most states regulate mutual funds whose shares are offered in those states.

Federal and state laws provide for appropriate disclosure to investors when it comes to potential returns and risks associated with individual funds. These laws are designed to ensure that mutual funds are operated and managed in the interests of their shareholders.

Taxation of Shareholders: Traditionally, an extra layer of taxation is avoided under the "conduit theory." Mutual fund shareholders are generally treated as if they directly held the securities in the fund's portfolio. Under Subchapter M of the Internal Revenue Code, qualified funds pay no federal income tax on their earnings and capital gains which are distributed to shareholders.

In order to qualify, a mutual fund has to distribute at least 90 percent of its investment company taxable income to its shareholders each year, among other requirements. Thus, a shareholder receives dividends and capital gains distributions from a qualifying fund without any tax being levied on the fund. Instead, shareholders report these payments on their own tax returns and pay the appropriate tax.

The Tax Reform Act of 1986 and subsequent legislation requires that a fund distribute 97 percent of its income from dividends and interest, and 98 percent of its net realized capital gains with respect to the calendar year in which they are earned or realized. The 1986 act also requires shareholders to be taxed on their share of a fund's gross income (income before fund expenses are subtracted), rather than on net distributions, beginning in 1987. This change would have imposed a tax on the "phantom income" imputed to shareholders, that is, income that shareholders never received but for which they were held accountable on their tax returns. However, in 1987 Congress ameliorated this harsh treatment by enacting legislation to delay the imposition of the phantom income tax on mutual fund shareholders for one year. In 1988, Congress expressed its intention to postpone the imposition of the phantom income tax for two more years until 1990, but through a drafting error in the legislation wound up repealing the phantom income tax entirely.

The Distribution of Mutual Funds

nvestors have a great deal of choice in the purchase of mutual funds. In addition to selecting among fund companies and fund types, they can choose from a growing number of avenues, or "distribution channels," through which to purchase mutual funds.

To learn how investors purchase mutual funds and what role the distribution channel plays in their purchases, the Investment Company Institute conducted an extensive study of recent buyers (defined as fund owners who had purchased long-term mutual funds between January 1984 and January 1988). Personal interviews were conducted with fund owners in 1,053 randomly

selected households throughout the United States.

Preliminary research found that fund investors used six main channels of distribution. Consequently, the study sampled investors who had purchased funds through at least one of the following channels: a full service broker/dealer, including both national and regional firms; an insurance agent; an independent financial planner not associated with a large brokerage or insurance company; a captive sales representative who sells only the investment products of one company; a direct marketer of mutual funds; or a deposit institution.

The research shows that mutual fund owners who purchased long-

Channels Used for Purchase of Mutual Funds*
January 1984 - December 1987
(percent of recent buyers)

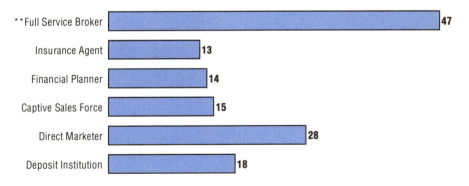

Channel	Percent
**Full Service Broker	47
Insurance Agent	13
Financial Planner	14
Captive Sales Force	15
Direct Marketer	28
Deposit Institution	18

* Multiple response

** Of all recent buyers, 47 percent purchased mutual funds through the full service broker channel

term mutual funds used full service brokers more frequently than any of the other distribution channels (47 percent of recent buyers). The second most frequently used channel is direct marketers (28 percent of recent buyers). In addition, the data show that the incidence of use of the remaining four channels--insurance agents, financial planners, captive sales force, and deposit institutions--is fairly evenly distributed during this period (between 13 and 18 percent of recent buyers).

The characteristics of recent buyers who use a particular distribution channel vary from channel to channel. For example, recent buyers who used a full service broker are, on average, slightly older and have a higher median income than other recent buyers. Their counterparts who bought through a direct marketer are younger, have among the highest income and financial asset levels, and own more long-term funds on average than do all recent buyers. Recent buyers who invested through independent financial planners have a lower amount of household financial

assets than other recent buyers, but one quarter of their assets are invested in mutual funds--the highest proportion of all recent buyers. These fund owners are also less likely to be retired than all other groups.

Recent buyers using a deposit institution for purchases of mutual funds are more likely to be female and retired. They have lower median incomes but higher amounts of financial assets; only 15 percent of their assets are invested in long-term mutual funds.

Recent buyers of mutual funds expressed many reasons for preferring one channel over another. In general, recent buyers attribute their use of a particular channel to one of three factors: the availability of advice, personalized service, and for some, the lower level of fees or charges associated with the fund purchase.

The importance of these factors varies depending on the channel used. For investors using an insurance agent, a captive sales representative, or a deposit institution for fund purchases, personalized service was

Selected Characteristics of Recent Fund Buyers*

	Median Age	Median Income	Average Share of Financial Assets in Long-term Funds	Average Number of Long-term Funds Owned	Retired
All Recent Buyers	48	$48,100	20%	2.6	18%
Channels Used:					
Full Service Broker	52	50,400	21	2.8	26
Insurance Agent	48	50,200	19	3.1	17
Financial Planner	49	47,500	25	3.4	11
Captive Sales Force	50	49,200	18	2.4	19
Direct Marketer	48	49,800	19	3.3	16
Deposit Institution	49	45,000	15	3.5	27

*Recent buyers purchased long-term mutual funds between January 1984 and January 1988.

cited as the most important reason to use these channels. Low or no fees associated with the fund purchase was of prime importance to recent buyers who used the direct marketer channel. The availability of initial and ongoing advice about investments was the most important channel attribute for buyers who used full service brokers.

Additional information on the way recent buyers use distribution channels for the purchase of mutual funds can be gleaned by examining the repeated use of a channel over time. This is referred to in the pie chart as the degree of loyalty to any one channel. One clear finding of the research is that two thirds of recent buyers made all of their fund investments through one channel. Eighty percent of recent buyers have used only one channel for at least three fourths of their mutual fund purchases. These figures represent an impressive

Overall Loyalty to Channel
(percent of recent buyers)

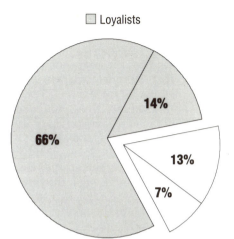

☐ Loyalists

66% Use One Channel for 100% of Mutual Fund Investments
14% Use One Channel for 75%-99% of Mutual Fund Investments
13% Use One Channel for 50%-74% of Mutual Fund Investments
7% Use One Channel for Less than 50% of Mutual Fund Investments

Distribution of Loyal Recent Buyers
(percentages)

Full Service Broker Channel	Insurance Agent Channel	Financial Planner Channel	Captive Sales Force Channel	Direct Marketer Channel	Deposit Institution
62	52	69	37	65	33

degree of recent buyer loyalty to the selected channel. On average, these investors made five purchases of long-term mutual funds during the period from January 1984 to January 1988.

Just as the demographic characteristics of recent buyers vary among the channels studied, the degree of loyalty shown to each channel varies as well. Loyalty, defined as more than 75 percent of an individual's fund purchases made through a single channel, is strongest for the financial planner, direct marketer, and full service broker/dealer channels. The strong relationship that exists between the buyer and the selling agent helps explain the loyalty shown to the financial planner, broker/dealer, and insurance agent channels. In the direct marketer channel, loyalty is related to cost considerations and to the willingness of recent buyers to make their own decisions.

The majority of recent buyers in the captive sales force and deposit institution channels have used more than one channel to purchase funds. Nevertheless, at least one third of those who purchased long-term mutual funds since 1984 were loyal to one of these channels. This pattern of limited loyalty is undoubtedly related to the narrower selection or more restricted availability of funds through these channels, particularly the deposit institution channel where mutual funds have not been widely available.

Since a clear majority of those surveyed indicated they would use the same channel for future mutual fund purchases, channel loyalty is likely to continue to be an important characteristic of fund owner behavior.

Glossary of Mutual Fund Terms

(For explanation of types of funds, see pages 9-10; for retirement plans, see page 44.)

Adviser
The organization employed by a mutual fund to give professional advice on the fund's investments and asset management practices (also called "investment adviser").

Asked or Offering Price
(As seen in some mutual fund newspaper listings.)
The price at which a mutual fund's shares can be purchased. The asked or offering price means the current net asset value per share plus sales charge, if any.

Automatic Reinvestment
An option available to mutual fund shareholders in which fund dividends and capital gains distributions are automatically plowed back into the fund to buy new shares and thereby increase holdings.

Bid or Redemption Price
(As seen in some mutual fund newspaper listings.)
The price at which a mutual fund's shares are redeemed (bought back) by the fund. The bid or redemption price usually equals the current net asset value per share.

Broker/Dealer (or Dealer)
A firm that buys and sells mutual fund shares and other securities to the public.

Capital Gains Distributions
Payments to mutual fund shareholders of profits realized on the sale of securities in the fund's portfolio. These amounts are usually distributed to shareholders annually.

Capital Growth
An increase in market value of a mutual fund's securities, as reflected in the net asset value of fund shares. This is a long-term objective of many mutual funds.

Captive (or Dedicated) Sales Force
See Sales Force Marketing.

Closed-end Investment Company
Unlike mutual funds (known as "open-end" investment companies), closed-end companies issue a limited number of shares and do not redeem them (buy them back). Instead, closed-end shares are traded in the securities markets, with supply and demand determining the price.

Contractual Plan
A program for the accumulation of mutual fund shares in which the investor agrees to invest a fixed amount on a regular basis for a specified number of years. A substantial portion of the sales charge applicable to the total investment is usually deducted from early payments.

Custodian
The organization (usually a bank) that keeps custody of securities and other assets of a mutual fund.

Direct Marketing
A method of distribution whereby funds sell their shares directly to the public without the intervention of a salesperson. Investors purchase fund shares through the mail or by telephone in response to advertising or direct solicitation.

Diversification
The mutual fund policy of spreading its investments among a number of different securities to reduce the risks inherent in investing. The average investor would find it difficult to amass a portfolio as diversified as that of a mutual fund.

Dollar-cost Averaging
Investing equal amounts of money at regular intervals regardless of whether securities markets are moving up or down. This practice reduces average share costs to the investor who acquires more shares in periods of lower securities prices and fewer shares in periods of higher prices. Unlike a contractual plan, dollar-cost averaging is voluntary.

Exchange Privilege
Enables mutual fund shareholders to transfer their investment from one fund to another within the same fund family as shareholder needs or objectives change. Usually funds let investors use the exchange privilege several times a year for a low or no fee per exchange.

Income Dividends
Payments to mutual fund shareholders of dividends, interest, and/or short-term capital gains earned on the fund's portfolio of securities after deducting operating expenses.

Investment Adviser
See Adviser.

Investment Company
A corporation, trust, or partnership which invests pooled funds of shareholders in securities appropriate to the fund's objective. Among the benefits of investment companies are professional management and diversification. Mutual funds ("open-end" investment companies) are the most popular type of investment company.

Investment Objective
The goal--such as long-term capital growth, current income, growth and income, etc.--which an investor or a mutual fund pursues. Each fund's objective is stated in its prospectus.

Load--no-load, front-end load, or back-end load
See Sales Charge.

Long-term Funds
An industry designation for all funds other than short-term funds (money market and short-term municipal bond). The two broad categories of long-term funds are equity (stock) and bond and income funds.

Management Fee
The amount paid by mutual funds to their investment advisers. The average annual fee industrywide is about one-half of one percent of fund assets.

Money Manager
See Portfolio Manager.

Mutual Fund
An investment company that pools money from shareholders and invests in a variety of securities, including stocks, bonds, and money market securities. A mutual fund stands ready to buy back (redeem) its shares at their current net asset value. The value of the shares depends on the market value of the fund's portfolio securities at the time. Most mutual funds offer new shares continuously.

National Association of Securities Dealers, Inc. (NASD)

A self-regulating organization for member securities firms with authority over the distribution of mutual fund shares and over-the-counter securities transactions.

Net Asset Value (NAV) Per Share

The market worth of a mutual fund's total assets--securities, cash, and any accrued earnings--after deducting liabilities, divided by the number of shares outstanding. NAV is expressed as the value of a single share in the fund.

Open-end Investment Company

The statutory terminology for a mutual fund, indicating that it stands ready to redeem (buy back) its shares on demand.

Over-the-Counter Market

The market for securities transactions conducted through a communications network connecting dealers in stocks and bonds. The rules of such trading are written and enforced by the National Association of Securities Dealers, Inc. (NASD), the same organization that provides self-policing of member firms in the distribution of mutual fund shares.

Payroll Deduction Plan

An arrangement some employers offer whereby employees may accumulate shares in a mutual fund. Employees authorize their employer to deduct a specified amount from their salary at stated times and transfer the proceeds to the fund.

Periodic Payment Plan

See Contractual Plan.

Portfolio Manager

Specialist employed by mutual fund companies to invest the pool of money in accordance with the fund's investment objectives.

Prospectus

The official booklet that describes a mutual fund. The prospectus contains information as required by the U.S. Securities and Exchange Commission on such subjects as the fund's investment objectives and policies, services, investment restrictions, officers and directors, how shares are bought and redeemed, fund fees and other charges, and the fund's financial statements.

Redemption Price

The amount per share that mutual fund shareholders receive when they liquidate their shares (also known as the "bid price").

Reinvestment Privilege

A service provided by most mutual funds for the automatic reinvestment of shareholder dividends and capital gains distributions into additional shares.

Sales Charge

An amount charged to purchase shares in many mutual funds sold by brokers or other members of a sales force. Typically, the charge ranges from 4 to 8.5 percent of the initial investment. The charge is added to the net asset value per share when determining the offering price.

Some funds sold by brokers and other sales personnel no longer charge the load "up front;" instead they charge an annual 12b-1 fee (see page 58), which may range up to 1.25 percent. In many cases, such funds also have a declining contingent-deferred sales charge, or "back-end load," on shares that are sold during the first few years of ownership. Funds that are sold directly to investors charge small commissions, or none at all. The latter are referred to as "no-load" funds.

Sales Force Marketing

A method of distribution whereby funds sell their shares to the public through sales professionals, such as brokers, financial planners, and insurance agents. Some fund organizations sell shares through a *captive sales force*, sales professionals employed by the fund organization to market only the shares of its associated funds.

Securities and Exchange Commission (SEC)

The primary U.S. federal agency that regulates investment companies.

Short-term Funds

An industry designation for money market and short-term municipal bond funds. Due to the special nature of these funds and the huge, continuous inflows and outflows of money they experience, they are rarely viewed in terms of sales figures, as long-term funds are. Tracking changes in total assets is usually the preferred method of following trends in short-term funds.

Transfer Agent

The organization employed by a mutual fund to prepare and maintain records relating to the accounts of its shareholders.

12b-1 Fee

Fee charged by some funds and named after the 1980 Securities and Exchange Commission rule that permits them. Such fees pay for distribution costs such as advertising or for commissions paid to brokers. The fund's prospectus details 12b-1 charges, if applicable.

Underwriter

The organization that acts as the distributor of a mutual fund's shares to broker/dealers and investors.

Unit Investment Trust

An investment company that purchases a fixed portfolio of income-producing securities. Units in the trust are sold to investors by brokers.

Variable Annuity

An investment contract sold to an investor by an insurance company. Capital is accumulated, often through investment in a mutual fund, and converted to an income stream at a future date, perhaps retirement. Income payments vary with the value of the account.

Withdrawal Plan

A program in which shareholders receive payments from their mutual fund investments at regular intervals. Typically, these payments are drawn from the fund's dividends and capital gains distributions, if any, and from principal, as needed. Many mutual funds offer these plans.

Data

Table of Contents

Section III:
Short-term Funds
(Money Market and Short-term Municipal Bond Funds)

Assets

Accounts

Section IV:
Exchanges for All Funds

Section V:
Retirement Plans

Section VI:
Institutional Investors

Accounts

Assets

Total Industry Assets
(billions of dollars)

Year	Equity, Bond, and Income Funds	Money Market Funds and Short-term Municipal Bond Funds	Total
1975	$42.2	$3.7	$45.9
1976	47.6	3.7	51.3
1977	45.0	3.9	48.9
1978	45.0	10.9	55.9
1979	49.0	45.2	94.2
1980	58.4	76.3	134.7
1981	55.2	186.1	241.3
1982	76.8	219.8	296.6
1983	113.6	179.3	293.0
1984	137.1	233.5	370.7
1985	251.7	243.8	495.5
1986	424.2	292.1	716.3
1987	453.8	316.1	769.9
1988	472.3	338.0	810.3

Total Industry Shareholder Accounts

(millions)

Year	Equity, Bond, and Income Funds	Money Market Funds and Short-term Municipal Bond Funds	Total
1975	9.7	0.2	9.9
1976	8.9	0.2	9.1
1977	8.5	0.2	8.7
1978	8.2	0.5	8.7
1979	7.5	2.3	9.8
1980	7.3	4.8	12.1
1981	7.2	10.3	17.5
1982	8.2	13.2	21.4
1983	12.1	12.5	24.6
1984	14.4	13.8	28.2
1985	20.0	15.0	35.0
1986	29.8	16.3	46.1
1987	36.9R	17.7	54.6R
1988	36.0	18.7	54.7

R--Revised

Total Number of Funds

Year	Equity, Bond, and Income Funds	Money Market Funds and Short-term Municipal Bond Funds	Total
1975	390	36	426
1976	404	48	452
1977	427	50	477
1978	444	61	505
1979	448	76	524
1980	458	106	564
1981	486	179	665
1982	539	318	857
1983	653	373	1,026
1984	820	426	1,246
1985	1,071	460	1,531
1986	1,356	487	1,843
1987	1,780	543	2,323
1988	2,111	607	2,718

An Overview:
Shareholder Accounts,
Total Net Assets, and Liquid Assets
Equity, Bond, and Income Funds
1970-1988

Calendar Yearend	Number of Reporting Funds	Number of Accounts (Thousands)	Net Assets (billions of dollars)	Liquid Assets (billions of dollars)
1970	361	10,690.3	$47.6	$3.1
1971	392	10,901.0	55.0	2.6
1972	410	10,635.3	59.8	2.6
1973	421	10,330.9	46.5	3.4
1974	416	9,970.4	34.1	3.4
1975	390	9,712.5	42.2	3.2
1976	404	8,879.4	47.6	2.4
1977	427	8,515.1	45.0	3.3
1978	444	8,190.6	45.0	4.5
1979	446	7,482.2	49.0	4.7
1980	458	7,325.5	58.4	5.3
1981	486	7,175.5	55.2	5.3
1982	539	8,190.3	76.8	6.0
1983	653	12,065.0	113.6	8.3
1984	820	14,471.3	137.1	12.2
1985	1,071	19,845.6	251.7	20.6
1986	1,356	29,790.2	424.2	30.7
1987	1,781	36,971.1	453.8	38.0
1988	2,111	36,012.8	472.3	45.1

Note: *Figures for shareholder accounts represent combined totals for member companies. Duplications have not been eliminated.*

Comparable data for short-term funds can be found on page 86. Industry totals can be found on pages 62-63.

Type of Shareholder Accounts
Equity, Bond, and Income Funds
1971-1988
(thousands)

Yearend	Total Shareholder Accounts	Regular Accounts	Contractual Accumulation Plans	Contractual Single Payment Plans	Withdrawal Accounts
Number					
1971	10,901	8,996	1,455	169	281
1972	10,635	8,856	1,342	157	280
1973	10,331	8,699	1,214	166	252
1974	9,970	8,524	1,081	140	225
1975	9,667	8,302	1,029	126	210
1976	8,879	7,647	930	112	190
1977	8,515	7,395	844	101	175
1978	8,068	7,080	757	75	156
1979	7,482	6,602	677	64	139
1980	7,326	6,598	554	45	129
1981	7,175	6,486	537	30	122
1982	8,190	7,573	471	28	118
1983	12,065	11,326	585	20	134
1984	14,424	13,666	615	17	126
1985	19,846	19,008	647	17	174
1986	29,790	28,919	624	16	231
1987	36,971	36,003	687	17	264
1988	36,013	35,132	605	16	260
Percent					
1971	100.0%	82.5%	13.3%	1.6%	2.6%
1972	100.0	83.3	12.6	1.5	2.6
1973	100.0	84.2	11.8	1.6	2.4
1974	100.0	85.5	10.8	1.4	2.3
1975	100.0	85.9	10.6	1.3	2.2
1976	100.0	86.1	10.5	1.3	2.1
1977	100.0	86.9	9.9	1.2	2.0
1978	100.0	87.8	9.4	0.9	1.9
1979	100.0	88.2	9.0	0.9	1.9
1980	100.0	90.1	7.6	0.6	1.7
1981	100.0	90.4	7.5	0.4	1.7
1982	100.0	92.5	5.8	0.3	1.4
1983	100.0	93.8	4.9	0.2	1.1
1984	100.0	94.8	4.2	0.1	0.9
1985	100.0	95.8	3.2	0.1	0.9
1986	100.0	97.0	2.1	0.1	0.8
1987	100.0	97.4	1.8	0.1	0.7
1988	100.0	97.6	1.7	0.0	0.7

Total Net Assets of Equity, Bond, and Income Funds by Fund Characteristics Yearend

(millions of dollars)

	1987		1988	
	Dollars	**Percent**	**Dollars**	**Percent**
Total Net Assets	**$453,842.4**	**100.0%**	**$472,296.6**	**100.0%**
Method of Sale				
Sales Force	$331,752.8	73.1%	$336,184.0	71.2%
Direct Marketing	107,496.1	23.7	120,728.6	25.5
Variable Annuity	12,730.1	2.8	13,592.8	2.9
Not Offering Shares	1,863.4	0.4	1,791.2	0.4
Investment Objective				
Aggressive Growth	$27,298.1	6.0%	$29,452.3	6.2%
Growth	48,037.6	10.6	50,547.2	10.7
Growth & Income	64,032.5	14.1	70,865.3	15.0
Precious Metals	4,050.9	0.9	3,171.9	0.7
International	6,982.3	1.5	6,831.8	1.4
Global Equity	10,449.2	2.3	11,151.1	2.4
Income-equity	14,745.1	3.3	17,509.5	3.7
Option/Income	5,095.2	1.1	5,286.3	1.1
Flexible Portfolio	4,287.2	1.0	3,485.7	0.7
Balanced	9,024.7	2.0	9,492.9	2.0
Income-mixed	11,418.4	2.5	8,768.7	1.9
Income-bond	12,580.0	2.8	10,693.3	2.3
U.S. Government Income	88,906.2	19.6	82,688.1	17.5
Ginnie Mae	34,204.0	7.5	28,712.0	6.1
Global Bond	2,137.1	0.5	3,024.3	0.6
Corporate Bond	9,470.5	2.1	10,463.9	2.2
High-yield Bond	24,157.2	5.3	33,425.2	7.1
Long-term Municipal Bond	49,174.6	10.8	54,316.3	11.5
State Municipal Bond, Long-term	27,791.6	6.1	32,410.8	6.9

Liquid Assets of Equity, Bond, and Income Funds by Fund Characteristics Yearend

(millions of dollars)

	1987		1988	
	Dollars	**Percent**	**Dollars**	**Percent**
Net Cash & Equivalent	**$38,006.1**	**100.0%**	**$45,089.5**	**100.0%**
Method of Sale				
Sales Force	$28,559.4	75.1%	$33,192.5	73.6%
Direct Marketing	7,856.6	20.7	10,107.6	22.4
Variable Annuity	1,438.7	3.8	106.3	0.3
Not Offering Shares	151.4	0.4	1,683.1	3.7
Investment Objective				
Aggressive Growth	$2,515.6	6.6%	$2,916.5	6.5%
Growth	5,216.5	13.7	5,492.4	12.2
Growth & Income	5,124.7	13.5	6,662.0	14.8
Precious Metals	380.3	1.0	296.1	0.6
International	352.9	0.9	417.8	0.9
Global Equity	1,643.9	4.3	860.2	1.9
Income-equity	1,086.1	2.9	1,114.4	2.5
Option/Income	261.7	0.7	578.4	1.3
Flexible Portfolio	814.0	2.1	777.5	1.7
Balanced	843.1	2.2	810.8	1.8
Income-mixed	883.9	2.3	907.9	2.0
Income-bond	1,407.4	3.7	1,894.2	4.2
U.S. Government Income	8,847.8	23.3	11,601.9	25.7
Ginnie Mae	1,258.3	3.3	1,210.8	2.7
Global Bond	474.2	1.3	522.9	1.2
Corporate Bond	749.8	2.0	1,368.2	3.0
High-yield Bond	1,760.0	4.6	2,328.1	5.2
Long-term Municipal Bond	3,184.5	8.4	3,915.1	8.7
State Municipal Bond, Long-term	1,201.4	3.2	1,414.3	3.1

Total Net Assets of Mutual Funds by Investment Objective Within Method of Sales 1985-1988

(millions of dollars)

Sales Force

	1985	1986	1987	1988
Aggressive Growth	$8,107.2	$9,024.4	$10,088.6	$9,867.4
Growth	22,479.9	28,245.5	30,940.1	30,501.1
Growth & Income	24,156.3	34,262.1	38,985.8	43,293.6
Precious Metals	975.4	1,223.9	2,415.7	1,983.8
International	701.1	2,097.0	2,608.0	2,761.7
Global Equity	5,172.8	7,944.1	10,248.3	10,940.7
Income-equity	2,718.3	5,478.9	6,321.7	7,388.3
Option/Income	5,493.5	6,835.1	4,863.3	5,255.3
Flexible Portfolio	853.3	1,213.8	3,720.9	2,840.9
Balanced	2,807.0	5,376.4	6,136.0	5,934.5
Income-mixed	5,283.5	8,054.1	9,179.0	6,651.3
Income-bond	3,793.1	7,433.9	8,633.2	7,389.3
U.S. Government Income	39,092.3	78,838.7	86,069.3	79,729.9
Ginnie Mae	15,715.7	31,866.6	27,490.3	22,310.5
Global Bond	64.4	453.2	1,589.2	2,480.8
Corporate Bond	4,294.0	7,735.6	8,055.6	7,078.5
High-yield Bond	11,025.5	19,612.3	19,922.6	28,005.7
Long-term Municipal Bond	15,273.6	29,782.6	32,782.7	37,020.5
State Municipal Bond, Long-term	8,404.9	19,159.2	21,702.5	24,750.2
Total	**$176,411.8**	**$304,637.4**	**$331,752.8**	**$336,184.0**

Direct Marketing

	1985	1986	1987	1988
Aggressive Growth	$11,482.1	$15,321.1	$16,527.7	$18,948.4
Growth	9,928.6	11,633.2	12,604.7	15,322.9
Growth & Income	13,525.8	18,333.5	19,810.6	21,974.3
Precious Metals	522.4	801.7	1,632.3	1,184.0
International	1,785.0	5,089.2	4,355.5	4,044.0
Global Equity	0.0	41.0	190.3	199.1
Income-equity	4,004.8	7,078.5	8,393.3	10,058.5
Option/Income	108.6	111.5	226.2	27.0
Flexible Portfolio	34.1	175.5	370.4	370.6
Balanced	1,266.7	2,070.6	2,780.2	3,498.6
Income-mixed	1,653.9	2,038.0	2,044.3	1,996.5
Income-bond	2,048.9	3,195.2	3,051.4	2,351.8
U.S. Government Income	1,152.0	3,132.2	2,242.6	2,419.6
Ginnie Mae	1,892.7	7,164.4	6,044.3	5,762.2
Global Bond	0.0	70.0	547.9	542.1
Corporate Bond	486.0	886.5	951.0	2,703.3
High-yield Bond	1,905.9	4,039.0	3,242.2	4,369.3
Long-term Municipal Bond	12651.1	20,074.6	16,392.0	17,295.8
State Municipal Bond, Long-term	3,114.6	6,655.6	6,089.2	7,660.6
Total	**$67,563.2**	**$107,911.3**	**$107,496.1**	**$120,728.6**

Distribution of Mutual Fund Assets in Equity, Bond, and Income Funds Yearend, 1970-1988

(millions of dollars)

Year	Total Net Assets	Net Cash & Equivalent	Corporate Bonds	Preferred Stocks	Common Stocks	Municipal Bonds	Long-term U.S. Gov't	Other
1970	$47,618	$3,124	$4,286	$1,143	$38,540	NA	NA	$525
1971	55,045	2,601	4,910	1,206	45,891	NA	NA	437
1972	59,831	2,598	5,068	993	50,735	NA	NA	437
1973	46,519	3,426	4,196	623	37,698	NA	NA	576
1974	34,062	3,357	3,611	426	26,103	NA	NA	565
1975	42,179	3,209	4,766	506	33,158	NA	NA	540
1976	47,582	2,352	6,977	655	37,158	NA	NA	440
1977	45,049	3,274	6,475	418	30,746	$2,256	$1,295	585
1978	44,980	4,507	5,545	405	30,678	2,550	1,093	202
1979	48,980	4,995	5,582	443	34,334	2,651	798	177
1980	58,400	5,321	6,582	531	41,561	2,866	1,433	106
1981	55,207	5,277	7,489	399	36,649	3,046	2,147	200
1982	76,841	6,040	10,833	1,628	47,720	6,797	3,752	71
1983	113,599	8,343	13,052	1,474	72,942	13,368	3,894	526
1984	137,126	11,978	15,018	1,627	81,597	18,522	8,009	375
1985	251,695	20,607	24,961	3,773	119,698	38,339	43,471	846
1986	424,156	30,716	47,310	7,387	153,657	70,875	111,536	2,675
1987	453,842	38,006	41,661	5,566	176,372	68,578	119,854	3,805
1988	472,297	45,090	54,441	5,678	173,684	86,136	103,750	3,518

Percent

Year	Total Net Assets	Net Cash & Equivalent	Corporate Bonds	Preferred Stocks	Common Stocks	Municipal Bonds	Long-term U.S. Gov't	Other
1970	100.0%	6.6%	9.0%	2.4%	80.9%	NA	NA	1.1%
1971	100.0	4.7	8.9	2.2	83.4	NA	NA	0.8
1972	100.0	4.3	8.5	1.7	84.8	NA	NA	0.7
1973	100.0	7.4	9.0	1.2	81.0	NA	NA	1.3
1974	100.0	9.9	10.6	1.2	76.6	NA	NA	1.7
1975	100.0	7.6	11.3	1.2	78.6	NA	NA	1.3
1976	100.0	4.9	14.7	1.4	78.1	NA	NA	0.9
1977	100.0	7.3	14.4	0.9	68.2	5.0%	2.9%	1.3
1978	100.0	10.0	12.3	0.9	68.2	5.7	2.4	0.5
1979	100.0	10.2	11.4	0.9	70.1	5.4	1.6	0.4
1980	100.0	9.1	11.3	0.9	71.2	4.9	2.4	0.2
1981	100.0	9.5	13.6	0.7	66.4	5.5	3.9	0.4
1982	100.0	7.9	14.1	2.1	62.1	8.8	4.9	0.1
1983	100.0	7.3	11.5	1.3	64.2	11.8	3.4	0.5
1984	100.0	8.7	11.0	1.2	59.5	13.5	5.8	0.3
1985	100.0	8.2	9.9	1.5	47.6	15.2	17.3	0.3
1986	100.0	7.3	11.2	1.7	36.2	16.7	26.3	0.6
1987	100.0	8.4	9.2	1.2	38.9	15.1	26.4	0.8
1988	100.0	9.5	11.5	1.2	36.8	18.2	22.0	0.8

An Overview: Sales, Redemptions, and Net Sales of Equity, Bond, and Income Funds
1970-1988
(millions of dollars)

Year	Sales	Redemptions	Net Sales
1970	$4,625.8	$2,987.6	$1,638.2
1971	5,147.2	4,750.2	397.0
1972	4,892.5	6,562.9	(1,670.4)
1973	4,359.3	5,651.1	(1,291.8)
1974	3,091.5	3,380.9	(289.4)
1975	3,307.2	3,686.3	(379.1)
1976	4,360.5	6,801.2	(2,440.7)
1977	6,399.6	6,026.0	373.6
1978	6,705.3	7,232.4	(527.1)
1979	6,826.1	8,005.0	(1,178.9)
1980	9,993.7	8,200.0	1,793.7
1981	9,710.4	7,470.4	2,240.0
1982	15,738.3	7,571.8	8,166.5
1983	40,325.1	14,677.6	25,647.5
1984	45,856.8	20,030.1	25,826.7
1985	114,313.5	33,763.3	80,550.2
1986	215,847.9	67,012.7	148,835.2
1987	190,628.0R	116,224.3	74,403.7R
1988	95,292.9	92,474.1	2,818.8

Comparable data for short-term funds can be found on pages 87-88.
R--Revised

Sales of Equity, Bond, and Income
Funds by Fund Characteristics
(millions of dollars)

	1987		1988	
	Dollars	**Percent**	**Dollars**	**Percent**
Sales	**$190,628.0R**	**100.0%**	**$95,292.9**	**100.0%**
Type of Sales				
Regular Single Payment	$171,054.7R	89.7%	$77,214.0	81.0%
Contractual Accumulation Plan	469.3	0.2	433.2	0.5
Contractual Single Payment	118.5	0.1	109.4	0.1
Reinvested Investment Income	18,985.5	10.0	17,536.3	18.4
Method of Sales				
Sales Force	$132,015.3	69.3%	$65,025.8	68.3%
Direct Marketing	53,091.0R	27.8	27,179.9	28.5
Variable Annuity	5,501.0	2.9	3,068.1	3.2
Not Offering Shares	20.7	0.0	19.1	0.0
Investment Objective				
Aggressive Growth	$11,756.0R	6.2%	$4,361.4	4.6%
Growth	17,723.5	9.3	8,386.3	8.8
Growth & Income	23,320.1	12.2	10,555.6	11.1
Precious Metals	3,180.8	1.7	1,193.3	1.3
International	4,183.6	2.2	1,214.4	1.3
Global Equity	3,130.4	1.6	1,348.4	1.4
Income-equity	6,760.2	3.5	3,088.3	3.2
Option/Income	2,011.1	1.1	866.5	0.9
Flexible Portfolio	2,966.3	1.6	1,075.8	1.1
Balanced	3,263.4	1.7	1,291.0	1.4
Income-mixed	5,915.5	3.1	2,714.3	2.8
Income-bond	5,400.6	2.8	3,634.1	3.8
U.S. Government Income	44,033.0	23.1	16,636.3	17.5
Ginnie Mae	13,251.1	7.0	4,548.8	4.8
Global Bond	1,118.7	0.6	1,509.0	1.6
Corporate Bond	3,683.5	1.9	2,289.5	2.4
High-yield Bond	10,020.1	5.3	9,828.2	10.3
Long-term Municipal Bond	17,991.2	9.4	12,626.2	13.2
State Municipal Bond, Long-term	10,918.9	5.7	8,125.5	8.5

R--Revised

Sales of Mutual Funds by Investment Objective Within Method of Sales 1985-1988

(millions of dollars)

Sales Force

Investment Objective	1985	1986	1987	1988
Aggressive Growth	$1,517.5	$2,380.5	$4,077.6	$1,576.9
Growth	4,751.2	7,697.4	10,508.8	4,781.4
Growth & Income	4,730.3	12,044.4	12,856.3	5,406.5
Precious Metals	223.5	204.6	1,277.5	345.2
International	198.8	1,048.5	1,988.8	571.8
Global Equity	1,088.3	3,088.5	3,076.4	1,291.0
Income-equity	1,104.6	2,640.6	3,175.3	1,671.1
Option/Income	2,708.7	3,041.0	1,710.3	710.0
Flexible Portfolio	138.1	344.5	2,610.9	784.3
Balanced	629.5	2,567.1	2,132.8	744.0
Income-mixed	3,197.6	5,335.9	4,723.4	1,996.9
Income-bond	1,202.7	3,628.7	3,767.7	2,395.9
U.S. Government Income	35,654.5	51,624.5	42,050.7	15,321.1
Ginnie Mae	11,765.1	24,930.1	9,710.8	3,198.7
Global Bond	25.7	407.6	775.3	1,201.7
Corporate Bond	1,384.8	3,808.4	2,875.6	1,307.9
High-yield Bond	4,665.3	10,541.5	7,012.8	7,508.6
Long-term Municipal Bond	6,753.9	15,441.4	10,371.1	8,696.2
State Municipal Bond, Long-term	4,686.0	10,802.4	7,313.3	5,516.6
Total	**$86,426.1**	**$161,577.6**	**$132,015.4**	**$65,025.8**

Direct Marketing

Investment Objective	1985	1986	1987	1988
Aggressive Growth	$5,125.2	$7,267.9	$7,309.4R	$2,558.5
Growth	2,050.3	3,624.6	5,723.8	2,675.5
Growth & Income	3,594.2	5,552.4	8,473.5	4,482.1
Precious Metals	385.3	452.0	1,900.5	845.9
International	562.3	3,121.4	2,192.6	636.8
Global Equity	0.3	22.6	50.3	40.9
Income-equity	1,179.5	2,829.5	3,584.2	1,414.6
Option/Income	64.0	61.8	300.5	156.2
Flexible Portfolio	30.2	142.6	232.4	156.2
Balanced	259.3	759.4	1,061.2	533.8
Income-mixed	733.1	1,345.9	1,112.1	684.6
Income-bond	847.7	1,518.0	1,387.7	1,007.1
U.S. Government Income	884.8	2,554.6	1,702.4	1,113.8
Ginnie Mae	1,281.7	3,660.0	3,301.7	1,220.7
Global Bond	0.0	31.6	343.4	306.5
Corporate Bond	152.9	368.0	579.7	759.9
High-yield Bond	1,051.1	2,993.7	2,610.1	2,047.9
Long-term Municipal Bond	5,875.7	9,218.7	7,620.0	3,930.0
State Municipal Bond, Long-term	2,108.3	4,417.0	3,605.5	2,608.9
Total	**$26,185.9**	**$49,941.7**	**$53,091.0R**	**$27,179.9**

R--Revised

Sales and Reinvested Dividends
by Fund Characteristics
1987-1988
(millions of dollars)

1987	Sales	Total Reinvested Dividends	Sales Less Reinvested Dividends
Total	**$190,628.0R**	**$19,008.9**	**$171,619.1**
Method of Sales			
Sales Force	$132,015.3	$14,297.5	$117,717.8
Direct Marketing	53,091.0	4,148.2	48,942.8
Variable Annuity	5,501.0	555.5	4,945.5
Not Offering Shares	20.7	7.7	13.0
Investment Objective			
Aggressive Growth	$11,756.0	$296.6	$11,459.4
Growth	17,723.5	1,675.0	16,048.5
Growth & Income	23,320.1	1,950.6	21,369.5
Precious Metals	3,180.8	85.2	3,095.6
International	4,183.6	179.7	4,003.9
Global Equity	3,130.4	305.8	2,824.6
Income-equity	6,760.2	342.5	6,417.7
Option/Income	2,011.1	309.3	1,701.8
Flexible Portfolio	2,966.3	178.3	2,788.0
Balanced	3,263.4	419.3	2,844.1
Income-mixed	5,915.5	607.9	5,307.6
Income-bond	5,400.6	790.8	4,609.8
U.S. Government Income	44,033.0	4,508.9	39,524.1
Ginnie Mae	13,251.1	1,758.0	11,493.1
Global Bond	1,118.7	46.0	1,072.7
Corporate Bond	3,683.5	459.7	3,223.8
High-yield Bond	10,020.1	1,735.6	8,284.5
Long-term Municipal Bond	17,991.2	2,349.5	15,641.7
State Municipal Bond, Long-term	10,918.9	1,010.2	9,908.7

1988			
Total	**$95,262.9**	**$17,536.3**	**$77,756.6**
Method of Sales			
Sales Force	$65,025.8	$13,125.2	$51,900.6
Direct Marketing	27,179.9	3,949.8	23,230.1
Variable Annuity	3,068.1	454.6	2,613.5
Not Offering Shares	19.1	6.7	12.4
Investment Objective			
Aggressive Growth	$4,361.4	$226.3	$4,135.1
Growth	8,386.3	1,223.3	7,163.0
Growth & Income	10,555.6	2,298.6	8,257.0
Precious Metals	1,193.3	55.6	1,137.7
International	1,214.4	106.6	1,107.8
Global Equity	1,348.4	250.6	1,097.8
Income-equity	3,088.3	317.9	2,770.4
Option/Income	866.5	250.5	616.0
Flexible Portfolio	1,075.8	104.9	970.9
Balanced	1,291.0	411.1	879.9
Income-mixed	2,714.3	488.5	2,225.8
Income-bond	3,634.1	693.7	2,940.4
U.S. Government Income	16,636.3	3,939.9	12,696.4
Ginnie Mae	4,548.8	1,305.7	3,243.1
Global Bond	1,509.0	160.8	1,348.2
Corporate Bond	2,289.5	551.6	1,737.9
High-yield Bond	9,828.2	1,972.5	7,855.7
Long-term Municipal Bond	12,626.2	2,156.7	10,469.5
State Municipal Bond, Long-term	8,125.5	1,021.5	7,104.0

R--Revised

Equity, Bond, and Income Funds' Distributions to Shareholders

(millions of dollars)

	Distributions from	
Year	Net Investment Income	Net Realized Capital Gains
1970	$1,414.1	$922.1
1971	1,330.7	775.5
1972	1,286.6	1,402.6
1973	1,300.2	943.3
1974	1,553.2	484.3
1975	1,449.1	219.2
1976	1,580.0	470.9
1977	1,789.7	634.8
1978	2,116.0	710.6
1979	2,451.4	929.9
1980	2,669.0	1,774.2
1981	3,143.0	2,697.2
1982	3,832.9	2,350.1
1983	4,981.0	4,391.6
1984	7,238.4	6,019.2
1985	12,864.2	4,984.6
1986	22,273.4	17,463.8
1987	31,823.7	22,975.6
1988	31,979.4	6,345.3

Annual Redemption Rate
for Equity, Bond, and Income Funds
1970-1988
(millions of dollars)

Year	Average Total Net Assets	Redemptions	Redemption Rate
1970	$47,954	$2,988	6.2%
1971	51,332	4,750	9.3
1972	57,438	6,563	11.4
1973	53,175	5,651	10.6
1974	40,290	3,381	8.4
1975	38,120	3,686	9.7
1976	44,880	6,801	15.2
1977	46,316	6,026	13.0
1978	45,014	7,232	16.4
1979	46,980	8,005	17.0
1980	53,690	8,200	15.3
1981	56,803	7,470	13.2
1982	66,024	7,572	11.5
1983	95,220	14,678	15.4
1984	125,362	20,030	16.0
1985	194,411	33,763	17.4
1986	337,926	67,013	19.8
1987	438,999	116,224	26.5
1988	463,070	92,474	20.0

Note: *"Average" Value Assets are an average of values at the beginning of the year and at the end of the year. The redemption rate is the dollar redemption volume as a percent of average assets.*

Redemptions of Equity, Bond, and Income Funds by Fund Characteristics

(millions of dollars)

	1987		1988	
	Dollars	**Percent**	**Dollars**	**Percent**
Redemptions	**$116,224.3**	**100.0%**	**$92,474.1**	**100.0%**
Type of Redemption				
Regular Account	$115,142.3	99.1%	$92,215.7	99.7%
Contractual Account	1,082.0	0.9	258.4	0.3
Method of Sales				
Sales Force	$81,528.4	70.1%	$67,324.5	72.8%
Direct Marketing	31,696.8	27.3	21,093.7	22.8
Variable Annuity	2,782.4	2.4	3,906.5	4.2
Not Offering Shares	216.7	0.2	149.4	0.2
Investment Objective				
Aggressive Growth	$7,210.9	6.2%	$5,202.5	5.6%
Growth	10,915.8	9.4	9,895.0	10.7
Growth & Income	10,961.1	9.4	10,972.7	11.9
Precious Metals	1,839.2	1.6	1,215.4	1.3
International	3,040.6	2.6	1,802.8	2.0
Global Equity	2,003.0	1.7	1,859.9	2.0
Income-equity	2,734.8	2.4	2,380.2	2.6
Option/Income	1,472.4	1.3	1,481.5	1.6
Flexible Portfolio	488.9	0.4	1,046.4	1.1
Balanced	1,112.2	1.0	1,664.9	1.8
Income-mixed	4,811.5	4.1	3,374.5	3.7
Income-bond	3,189.6	2.7	2,706.4	2.9
U.S. Government Income	27,406.4	23.6	20,890.2	22.6
Ginnie Mae	12,994.0	11.2	7,165.5	7.7
Global Bond	488.8	0.4	731.1	0.8
Corporate Bond	2,233.4	1.9	1,890.8	2.0
High-yield Bond	5,899.7	5.1	5,527.4	6.0
Long-term Municipal Bond	11,688.9	10.1	8,376.9	9.1
State Municipal Bond, Long-term	5,733.1	4.9	4,290.0	4.6

Redemptions of Mutual Funds by Investment Objective Within Method of Sales 1985-1988

(millions of dollars)

Sales Force

Investment Objective	1985	1986	1987	1988
Aggressive Growth	$1,488.8	$1,736.0	$2,621.8	$2,303.5
Growth	3,796.8	4,834.0	6,037.9	5,934.9
Growth & Income	2,452.5	4,680.8	6,211.9	6,333.6
Precious Metals	159.9	230.6	562.7	346.6
International	72.0	425.7	1,203.2	819.7
Global Equity	766.9	1,181.2	1,965.4	1,797.7
Income-equity	277.9	798.5	1,701.4	1,256.1
Option/Income	603.8	1,074.2	1,271.4	1,324.3
Flexible Portfolio	85.5	149.4	417.0	869.1
Balanced	197.7	360.6	777.1	1,277.1
Income-mixed	1,552.7	2,691.7	4,093.9	2,759.8
Income-bond	343.4	1,028.2	2,083.5	1,961.8
U.S. Government Income	4,653.9	13,308.3	26,124.7	19,955.0
Ginnie Mae	1,527.4	6,041.1	10,545.0	5,866.7
Global Bond	6.6	27.2	420.5	556.4
Corporate Bond	387.5	763.3	1,756.6	1,255.7
High-yield Bond	938.1	2,190.7	3,995.1	4,063.3
Long-term Municipal Bond	1,277.3	2,980.3	6,189.1	5,646.6
State Municipal Bond, Long-term	535.6	1,426.1	3,550.2	2,996.5
Total	**$21,124.3**	**$45,927.9**	**$81,528.4**	**$67,324.4**

Direct Marketing

Investment Objective	1985	1986	1987	1988
Aggressive Growth	$3,371.3	$3,441.6	$4,252.2	$2,531.9
Growth	1,735.8	2,664.4	3,919.3	2,812.4
Growth & Income	1,592.3	2,525.4	4,149.2	3,274.3
Precious Metals	321.6	452.7	1,275.8	868.3
International	260.5	1,320.3	1,836.7	980.6
Global Equity	0.0	0.7	21.3	49.7
Income-equity	221.3	590.8	1,033.3	1,122.7
Option/Income	54.3	29.1	199.8	155.9
Flexible Portfolio	14.5	19.1	47.4	102.3
Balanced	80.0	153.2	325.9	360.3
Income-mixed	301.1	503.4	684.4	581.5
Income-bond	315.6	577.2	936.5	604.0
U.S. Government Income	146.3	731.1	1,117.8	758.8
Ginnie Mae	97.4	875.6	2,284.2	1,106.3
Global Bond	0.0	0.6	68.3	174.6
Corporate Bond	35.7	69.7	286.8	479.2
High-yield Bond	188.9	803.1	1,575.2	1,107.4
Long-term Municipal Bond	2,035.3	3,400.7	5,499.7	2,730.3
State Municipal Bond, Long-term	449.7	1,249.9	2,183.0	1,293.4
Total	**$11,221.6**	**$19,408.6**	**$31,696.8**	**$21,093.9**

Sales of Equity, Bond, and Income Fund Shares by State and Geographical Regions Within Method of Sales
1988
(thousands of dollars)

	Sales Force	Direct Marketing	Total
New England	**$4,042,101**	**$3,461,111**	**$7,503,212**
Connecticut	1,267,375	503,674	1,771,049
Maine	171,749	114,161	285,910
Massachusetts	2,020,590	2,574,953	4,595,543
New Hampshire	226,660	111,550	338,210
Rhode Island	237,540	120,875	358,415
Vermont	118,187	35,898	154,085
Middle Atlantic	**$13,793,484**	**$5,909,261**	**$19,702,745**
New Jersey	3,367,522	1,139,959	4,507,481
New York	7,278,181	3,716,455	10,994,636
Pennsylvania	3,147,781	1,052,847	4,200,628
East North Central	**$10,383,510**	**$3,755,023**	**$14,138,533**
Illinois	3,146,272	1,297,928	4,444,200
Indiana	1,085,911	204,894	1,290,805
Michigan	2,319,504	666,311	2,985,815
Ohio	2,563,442	1,287,305	3,850,747
Wisconsin	1,268,381	298,585	1,566,966
West North Central	**$6,025,076**	**$1,234,154**	**$7,259,230**
Iowa	849,752	95,764	945,516
Kansas	654,943	146,854	801,797
Minnesota	1,735,635	424,347	2,159,982
Missouri	1,748,812	434,748	2,183,560
Nebraska	617,650	91,396	709,046
North Dakota	209,441	20,506	229,947
South Dakota	208,843	20,539	229,382
South Atlantic	**$8,305,750**	**$4,036,695**	**$12,342,445**
Delaware	149,349	62,913	212,262
District of Columbia	279,731	168,537	448,268
Florida	3,713,334	1,136,338	4,849,672
Georgia	814,217	364,942	1,179,159
Maryland	959,218	1,132,765	2,091,983
North Carolina	848,583	406,221	1,254,804
South Carolina	364,826	99,282	464,108
Virginia	973,533	616,360	1,589,893
West Virginia	202,959	49,337	252,296

Sales of Equity, Bond, and Income Fund Shares by State and Geographical Regions Within Method of Sales
1988
(thousands of dollars)

	Sales Force	Direct Marketing	Total
East South Central	**$1,960,921**	**$505,363**	**$2,466,284**
Alabama	463,099	107,574	570,673
Kentucky	515,405	145,215	660,620
Mississippi	218,252	50,456	268,708
Tennessee	764,165	202,118	966,283
West South Central	**$4,422,371**	**$1,932,414**	**$6,354,785**
Arkansas	349,152	57,135	406,287
Louisiana	603,628	124,401	728,029
Oklahoma	516,591	138,198	654,789
Texas	2,953,000	1,612,680	4,565,680
Mountain	**$3,929,362**	**$1,089,261**	**$5,018,623**
Arizona	969,191	337,808	1,306,999
Colorado	1,330,757	359,314	1,690,071
Idaho	222,606	39,822	262,428
Montana	265,140	24,359	289,499
Nevada	241,089	112,355	353,444
New Mexico	373,796	90,214	464,010
Utah	391,154	88,765	479,919
Wyoming	135,629	36,624	172,253
Pacific	**$11,711,298**	**$5,040,816**	**$16,752,114**
Alaska	89,274	36,920	126,194
California	9,366,752	4,124,066	13,490,818
Hawaii	172,045	80,803	252,848
Oregon	757,149	271,192	1,028,341
Washington	1,326,078	527,835	1,853,913
U.S. Territories & Possessions	**$49,338**	**$34,219**	**$83,557**
Canada	**$29,061**	**$14,436**	**$43,497**
Other Countries	**$373,396**	**$167,075**	**$540,471**
Total	**$65,025,668**	**$27,179,828**	**$92,205,496**

Sales of Equity, Bond, and Income Fund Shares
by State and Geographical Regions
Within Method of Sales
1988
(percent of total)

	Sales Force	Direct Marketing	Total
New England	**6.22%**	**12.73%**	**8.14%**
Connecticut	1.95	1.85	1.92
Maine	.26	.42	.31
Massachusetts	3.11	9.47	4.98
New Hampshire	.35	.41	.37
Rhode Island	.37	.45	.39
Vermont	.18	.13	.17
Middle Atlantic	**21.21%**	**21.74%**	**21.37%**
New Jersey	5.18	4.20	4.89
New York	11.19	13.67	11.92
Pennsylvania	4.84	3.87	4.56
East North Central	**15.97%**	**13.82%**	**15.33%**
Illinois	4.84	4.78	4.82
Indiana	1.67	.75	1.40
Michigan	3.57	2.45	3.24
Ohio	3.94	4.74	4.17
Wisconsin	1.95	1.10	1.70
West North Central	**9.27%**	**4.54%**	**7.87%**
Iowa	1.31	.35	1.02
Kansas	1.01	.54	.87
Minnesota	2.67	1.56	2.34
Missouri	2.69	1.60	2.37
Nebraska	.95	.34	.77
North Dakota	.32	.07	.25
South Dakota	.32	.08	.25
South Atlantic	**12.77%**	**14.85%**	**13.39%**
Delaware	.23	.23	.23
District of Columbia	.43	.62	.49
Florida	5.71	4.18	5.26
Georgia	1.25	1.34	1.28
Maryland	1.48	4.17	2.27
North Carolina	1.30	1.49	1.36
South Carolina	.56	.37	.50
Virginia	1.50	2.27	1.73
West Virginia	.31	.18	.27

Sales of Equity, Bond, and Income Fund Shares
by State and Geographical Regions
Within Method of Sales
1988
(percent of total)

	Sales Force	Direct Marketing	Total
East South Central	**3.02%**	**1.86%**	**2.67%**
Alabama	.71	.40	.62
Kentucky	.79	.53	.71
Mississippi	.34	.19	.29
Tennessee	1.18	.74	1.05
West South Central	**6.80%**	**7.11%**	**6.89%**
Arkansas	.54	.21	.44
Louisiana	.93	.46	.79
Oklahoma	.79	.51	.71
Texas	4.54	5.93	4.95
Mountain	**6.04%**	**4.01%**	**5.44%**
Arizona	1.49	1.24	1.42
Colorado	2.05	1.32	1.83
Idaho	.34	.15	.29
Montana	.41	.09	.31
Nevada	.37	.41	.38
New Mexico	.57	.33	.50
Utah	.60	.33	.52
Wyoming	.21	.14	.19
Pacific	**18.01%**	**18.55%**	**18.17%**
Alaska	.14	.14	.14
California	14.40	15.17	14.63
Hawaii	.27	.30	.27
Oregon	1.16	1.00	1.12
Washington	2.04	1.94	2.01
U.S. Territories & Possessions	**.08%**	**.13**	**.09%**
Canada	**.04%**	**.05%**	**.05%**
Other Countries	**.57%**	**.61%**	**.59%**
Total	**100.00%**	**100.00%**	**100.00%**

Total Purchases, Total Sales, and Net Purchases of Portfolio Securities by Mutual Funds 1970-1988

(millions of dollars)

Year	Total Purchases	Total Sales	Net Purchases
1970	$20,405.0	$18,588.5	$1,816.5
1971	25,360.2	24,793.8	566.4
1972	24,467.6	25,823.6	(1,356.0)
1973	19,706.6	21,903.0	(2,196.4)
1974	12,299.7	12,213.5	86.2
1975	15,396.9	15,511.4	(114.5)
1976	15,348.2	16,881.2	(1,533.0)
1977	18,168.0	19,420.7	(1,252.7)
1978	20,945.6	23,069.7	(2,124.1)
1979	22,412.1	23,702.5	(1,290.4)
1980	32,987.2	32,080.6	906.6
1981	36,161.7	33,709.2	2,452.5
1982	55,682.0	47,920.7	7,761.3
1983	93,009.5	71,466.5	21,543.0
1984	119,272.4	98,929.6	20,342.8
1985	259,578.5	186,974.6	72,603.9
1986	501,058.5	365,167.6	135,890.9
1987	531,075.8	485,640.1	45,435.7
1988	410,714.2	421,449.6	(10,735.4)

Note: *Parentheses indicate net portfolio sales.*

Total Purchases, Total Sales, and Net Purchases of Common Stocks by Mutual Funds 1970-1988

(millions of dollars)

Year	Total Purchases	Total Sales	Net Purchases
1970	$17,127.6	$15,900.8	$1,226.8
1971	21,557.7	21,175.1	382.6
1972	20,943.5	22,552.8	(1,609.3)
1973	15,560.7	17,504.4	(1,943.7)
1974	9,085.3	9,372.1	(286.8)
1975	10,948.7	11,902.3	(953.6)
1976	10,729.1	13,278.3	(2,549.2)
1977	8,704.7	12,211.3	(3,506.6)
1978	12,832.9	14,454.7	(1,621.8)
1979	13,089.0	15,923.0	(2,834.0)
1980	19,893.8	21,799.9	(1,906.1)
1981	20,859.7	21,278.3	(418.6)
1982	27,397.2	24,939.6	2,457.6
1983	54,581.7	40,813.9	13,767.8
1984	56,587.9	50,895.0	5,692.9
1985	80,783.1	72,577.3	8,205.8
1986	134,711.0	118,091.9	16,619.1
1987	199,042.0	176,084.9	22,957.1
1988	112,831.8	128,896.2	(16,064.4)

Note: *Parentheses indicate net portfolio sales.*

Total Purchases, Total Sales, and Net Purchases of Securities Other Than Common Stocks by Mutual Funds
1970-1988

(millions of dollars)

Year	Total Purchases	Total Sales	Net Purchases
1970	$3,277.4	$2,687.7	$589.7
1971	3,802.5	3,618.6	183.9
1972	3,524.1	3,270.9	253.2
1973	4,145.9	4,398.7	(252.8)
1974	3,214.4	2,841.4	373.0
1975	4,448.2	3,609.1	839.1
1976	4,619.1	3,602.9	1,016.2
1977	9,463.3	7,209.4	2,253.9
1978	8,112.7	8,615.0	(502.3)
1979	9,323.1	7,779.5	1,543.6
1980	13,093.4	10,280.7	2,812.7
1981	15,302.0	12,430.9	2,871.1
1982	28,284.8	22,981.1	5,303.7
1983	38,427.7	30,652.6	7,775.1
1984	62,684.6	48,034.6	14,650.0
1985	178,795.3	114,397.3	64,398.0
1986	366,347.5	247,075.7	119,271.8
1987	332,033.8	309,555.2	22,478.6
1988	297,882.5	292,553.5	5,329.0

Note: *Parentheses indicate net portfolio sales.*

Portfolio Purchases and Sales
by Fund Characteristics
(millions of dollars)

	1987		1988	
	Purchases	**Sales**	**Purchases**	**Sales**
All Securities	**$531,075.8**	**$485,640.1**	**$410,714.2**	**$421,449.6**
Method of Sale				
Sales Force	$380,253.3	$343,174.2	$291,932.3	$303,430.6
Direct Marketing	135,227.8	129,308.6	105,796.5	104,560.2
Not Offering Shares	15,318.7	12,815.4	304.4	306.2
Variable Annuity	276.0	341.9	12,681.0	13,152.6
Investment Objective				
Aggressive Growth	$43,000.0	$40,908.8	$26,513.5	$29,204.7
Growth	53,996.4	49,757.3	5,528.0	39,468.9
Growth & Income	62,631.5	50,891.6	35,370.4	39,049.4
Precious Metals	3,075.8	1,731.2	1,215.3	1,303.1
International	8,901.9	11,386.7	4,623.5	5,787.5
Global Equity	6,751.4	5,706.6	5,073.1	4,998.5
Income-equity	18,708.2	15,124.6	11,562.3	11,090.4
Option/income	13,938.9	14,140.8	3,867.6	5,326.4
Flexible Portfolio	9,841.8	7,629.1	6,407.8	6,656.3
Balanced	11,365.6	9,836.9	9,917.5	10,682.0
Income-mixed	13,450.6	12,681.7	8,036.3	8,912.1
Income-bond	13,964.5	12,451.6	13,064.9	12,488.4
U.S. Government Income	133,289.2	120,969.3	107,611.3	115,630.9
Ginnie Mae	41,718.0	41,804.8	42,003.5	43,473.6
Global Bond	3,571.6	2,247.8	6,864.8	6,025.8
Corporate Bond	10,029.2	9,105.6	8,588.2	8,553.0
High-yield Bond	25,397.9	24,209.6	25,882.1	21,371.7
Long-term Municipal Bond	40,932.6	40,525.5	40,130.6	36,373.4
State Municipal Bond, Long-term	16,510.7	14,530.6	18,453.5	15,053.5
Common Stock Only	**$199,042.0**	**$176,084.9**	**$112,831.8**	**$128,896.2**
Method of Sale				
Sales Force	$113,529.4	$98,997.6	$61,300.8	$72,737.7
Direct Marketing	77,494.8	70,807.7	46,541.0	50,187.9
Not Offering Shares	7,762.9	5,941.8	301.5	305.5
Variable Annuity	254.9	337.8	4,688.5	5,665.1
Investment Objective				
Aggressive Growth	$40,873.7	$38,563.5	24,653.1	27,829.1
Growth	51,865.3	48,051.2	34,111.8	38,407.7
Growth & Income	46,677.2	36,008.0	23,416.6	28,568.0
Precious Metals	2,933.4	1,634.1	882.5	977.1
International	8,249.7	10,909.3	4,185.9	4,841.2
Global Equity	6,366.4	5,362.1	4,651.5	4,600.7
Income-equity	13,751.4	10,238.5	1,482.2	8,411.5
Option/Income	13,625.0	14,007.9	3,038.8	4,887.4
Flexible Portfolio	4,499.6	2,833.2	3,112.0	3,237.6
Balanced	4,768.1	3,594.4	3,084.4	3,962.2
Income-mixed	3,556.4	3,573.0	1,482.2	1,826.7
Income-bond	588.3	510.9	13.5	21.2
U.S. Government Income	124.8	34.7	0.0	0.0
Ginnie Mae	0.0	0.0	0.0	0.0
Global Bond	301.2	110.6	11.9	368.1
Corporate Bond	195.3	42.0	59.8	29.6
High-yield Bond	663.8	611.5	1,141.1	928.1
Long-term Municipal Bond	0.0	0.0	0.0	0.0
State Municipal Bond, Long-term	2.4	0.0	0.0	0.0

Total Short-term Funds*
1980-1988
(millions of dollars)

Yearend	Total Sales	Total Redemptions	Net Sales	Number of Funds	Total Accounts Outstanding	Total Net Assets
1980	$237,427.7	$207,877.7	$29,550.0	106	4,762,103	$76,361.3
1981	462,422.6	354,972.1	107,450.5	179	10,323,466	186,158.2
1982	611,202.9	580,778.4	30,424.5	318	13,258,143	219,837.5
1983	507,447.0	551,151.3	(43,704.3)	373	12,539,688	179,386.5
1984	634,226.7	586,992.4	47,234.3	427	13,844,697	233,553.8
1985	839,498.8	831,121.2	8,377.6	460	14,954,726	243,802.4
1986	989,816.0	948,641.3	41,174.7	487	16,313,148	292,151.6
1987	1,060,949.2R	1,062,519.7R	(1,570.5)R	543	17,674,790	316,096.1
1988	1,081,702.0	1,074,373.5	7,328.5	606	18,720,186	337,956.5

*Figures are totals for money market and short-term municipal bond funds.

Comparable data for long-term funds can be found on page 64, 70.

R--Revised

An Overview: Money Market Funds*
1974-1988
(millions of dollars)

Yearend	Total Sales	Total Redemptions	Net Sales	Number of Funds	Total Accounts Outstanding	Average Maturity (days)	Total Net Assets
1974	$2,232.0	$556.0	$1,676.0	15	NA	NA	$1,715.1
1975	6,748.7	5,883.9	864.8	36	208,777	93	3,695.7
1976	9,360.0	9,609.2	(248.3)	48	180,676	110	3,685.8
1977	10,673.0	10,662.7	10.3	50	177,522	76	3,887.7
1978	30,452.2	24,294.5	6,157.7	61	467,803	42	10,858.0
1979	111,855.1	78,363.4	33,491.7	76	2,307,852	34	45,214.2
1980	232,172.8	204,068.5	28,104.3	96	4,745,572	24	74,447.7
1981	451,889.5	346,701.5	105,188.0	159	10,282,095	34	181,910.4
1982	581,758.9	559,581.1	22,177.8	281	13,101,347	37	206,607.5
1983	462,978.7	508,729.9	(45,751.2)	307	12,276,639	37	162,549.5
1984	571,959.3	531,050.9	40,908.4	329	13,556,180	43	209,731.9
1985	730,073.8	732,343.0	(2,269.2)	348	14,435,386	37	207,535.3
1986	792,349.1	776,303.2	16,045.9	360	15,653,595	40	228,345.8
1987	869,099.1R	865,668.4R	3,430.7R	389	16,832,666	31	254,676.4
1988	903,425.9	899,397.3	4,028.6	432	17,800,097	28	272,296.3

* A small percentage of funds report assets and liquid assets but not sales and redemptions. In the interest of comparability, these latter two sets of figures have been adjusted upward.

R--Revised

An Overview: Short-term Municipal Bond Funds
1980-1988
(millions of dollars)

Yearend	Total Sales	Total Redemptions	Net Sales	Number of Funds	Total Accounts Outstanding	Total Net Assets
1980	$5,254.9	$3,809.2	$1,445.7	10	16,531	$1,913.6
1981	10,533.1	8,270.6	2,262.5	20	41,371	4,247.8
1982	29,444.0	21,197.3	8,246.7	37	156,796	13,230.0
1983	44,468.3	42,421.4	2,046.9	66	263,049	16,837.0
1984	62,267.4	55,941.5	6,325.9	97	288,517	23,821.9
1985	109,425.0	98,778.2	10,646.8	112	499,245	36,267.1
1986						
National	188,017.3	165,329.1	22,688.2	101	604,055	59,367.5
State	9,449.7	7,009.1	2,440.6	26	55,498	4,438.2
1987						
National	179,215.0	185,031.1	(5,816.1)	112	731,265	54,555.8
State	12,635.1	11,820.2	814.9	42	110,859	6,863.9
1988						
National	158,085.8	158,120.8	(35.0)	120	744,955	54,541.7
State	20,190.4	16,855.5	3,334.9	54	175,134	11,118.5

Money Market Fund Monthly Assets
by Type of Fund
(thousands of dollars)

	General Purpose	Broker/Dealer	Institutional	Total
1986				
January	$60,287,636	$95,685,132	$54,642,661	$210,615,429
February	58,891,053	96,135,696	53,533,384	208,560,133
March	59,152,306	98,858,947	56,275,871	212,287,124
April	59,628,242	100,841,607	61,477,390	221,947,239
May	61,200,777	101,558,046	61,150,849	223,909,672
June	61,642,027	101,231,483	59,139,087	222,012,597
July	62,880,871	102,817,552	63,811,430	229,509,853
August	62,074,260	102,190,551	67,320,208	231,585,019
September	65,294,526	104,120,377	65,050,491	234,465,394
October	64,043,419	103,961,125	65,666,205	233,670,749
November	63,485,188	104,012,724	64,941,139	232,439,051
December	63,316,578	103,298,324	61,730,926	228,345,828
1987				
January	$60,988,081	$106,398,732	$65,091,719	$232,478,532
February	62,143,193	107,774,640	65,678,138	235,595,971
March	62,075,713	107,399,569	64,767,345	234,242,627
April	66,054,314	105,307,665	64,067,027	235,429,006
May	67,917,069	105,168,355	64,444,343	237,529,767
June	66,801,688	103,587,638	64,394,363	234,783,689
July	67,448,174	105,342,003	66,402,493	239,192,670
August	69,555,153	106,868,707	66,155,812	242,579,672
September	71,269,312	106,487,402	63,498,672	241,255,386
October	78,363,282	106,727,188	69,760,408	254,850,878
November	78,194,792	108,015,274	73,475,528	259,685,594
December	78,321,502	106,682,635	69,672,303	254,676,440
1988				
January	$79,551,417	$113,391,872	$79,432,998	$272,376,287
February	80,263,990	114,354,055	81,415,842	276,033,887
March	81,691,652	116,859,262	76,253,687	274,804,601
April	81,229,804	115,514,145	73,259,559	270,003,508
May	82,778,861	114,272,509	71,115,685	268,167,055
June	80,104,053	113,025,867	68,605,338	261,735,258
July	81,609,417	112,965,502	67,794,611	262,369,530
August	83,790,825	112,426,918	68,314,085	264,531,828
September	82,665,623	111,398,819	67,415,164	261,479,606
October	84,487,624	113,460,580	69,588,728	267,536,932
November	88,751,635	117,223,747	71,364,634	277,340,016
December	88,092,457	114,705,514	69,498,375	272,296,346

Money Market Fund Asset Composition
Yearend, 1983-1988
(millions of dollars)

	1983	1984	1985	1986	1987	1988
Total Net Assets	$162,549.5	$209,731.9	$207,535.3	$228,345.8	$254,676.4	$272,296.3
U.S. Treasury Bills	20,484.0	20,197.9	20,391.5	20,428.6	4,944.0	5,110.2
Other Treasury Securities	2,354.6	5,214.7	4,271.9	7,602.9	9,358.6	6,448.4
Other U.S. Securities	13,375.2	16,974.3	18,043.1	15,120.3	26,998.9	18,377.0
Repurchase Agreements	13,028.5	22,769.8	26,068.6	32,160.1	39,290.6	41,677.1
Commercial Bank CDs (1)	18,931.3	18,362.5	13,256.3	13,427.2	24,216.9	26,601.3
Other Domestic CDs (2)	5,107.4	5,270.7	3,578.5	5,684.3	9,333.7	6,151.1
Eurodollar CDs (3)	21,911.1	21,213.5	19,027.0	22,168.4	21,611.7	29,694.8
Commercial Paper	46,752.6	78,408.1	87,555.4	94,882.0	100,534.4	117,055.7
Bankers' Acceptances	19,586.2	19,564.2	11,578.3	10,405.7	10,771.2	12,035.8
Cash Reserves	(274.5)	(1,244.5)	154.8	(24.9)	(326.7)	664.6
Other	1,293.1	3,000.7	3,609.9	6,491.2	7,943.1	8,480.3
Average Maturity (4)	37	43	37	40	31	28
Number of Funds	307	329	348	360	389	432

(1) Commercial bank CDs are those issued by American banks located in the U.S.

(2) Other Domestic CDs include those issued by S&Ls and American branches of foreign banks.

(3) Eurodollar CDs are those issued by foreign branches of domestic banks and some issued by Canadian banks; this category includes some one day paper.

(4) Maturity of each individual security in the portfolio at end of month weighted by its value.

Comparable data for long-term funds can be found on page 69.

Money Market Fund
Shareholder Accounts by Type of Fund

	General Purpose	Broker/Dealer	Institutional	Total
1986				
January	4,755,720	9,593,273	137,829	14,486,822
February	4,815,685	9,701,239	134,022	14,650,946
March	4,912,296	9,902,169	137,049	14,951,514
April	4,967,756	10,345,979	141,512	15,455,247
May	4,958,173	10,336,859	145,785	15,440,817
June	4,965,974	10,380,050	144,306	15,490,330
July	4,963,533	10,471,572	143,511	15,578,616
August	4,937,707	10,483,803	143,362	15,564,872
September	4,993,508	10,554,627	144,976	15,693,111
October	4,982,390	10,572,966	136,604	15,691,960
November	4,932,956	10,579,632	134,509	15,647,097
December	4,889,141	10,623,590	140,864	15,653,595
1987				
January	4,797,360	10,723,207	143,019	15,663,586
February	4,799,661	10,763,009	141,378	15,704,048
March	4,788,670	10,912,577	138,327	15,839,574
April	4,947,334	11,208,138	140,922	16,296,394
May	4,979,964	11,288,344	142,921	16,411,229
June	4,962,648	11,181,233	144,033	16,287,914
July	4,981,636	11,213,898	128,857	16,324,391
August	4,986,780	11,294,936	124,558	16,406,274
September	5,039,203	11,541,156	125,241	16,705,600
October	5,227,676	11,437,447	141,938	16,807,061
November	5,529,616	11,361,473	139,240	16,760,329
December	5,266,231	11,422,519	143,916	16,832,666
1988				
January	5,250,695	11,526,458	146,355	16,923,508
February	5,320,637	11,518,521	146,957	16,986,115
March	5,385,371	11,673,362	136,511	17,195,244
April	5,416,521	11,897,794	139,925	17,454,240
May	5,401,893	11,644,054	137,431	17,183,378
June	5,376,975	11,595,112	137,679	17,109,766
July	5,278,864	11,334,498	142,242	16,755,604
August	5,253,919	11,470,376	139,194	16,863,489
September	5,328,210	11,530,103	139,198	16,997,511
October	5,267,584	11,725,059	140,364	17,133,007
November	5,611,963	11,997,068	139,237	17,748,268
December	5,576,656	12,076,897	146,544	17,800,097

Sales Due to Exchanges by Investment Objective
1987-1988
(millions of dollars)

Investment Objective	1987	1988
Aggressive Growth	$28,267.5	$17,855.7
Growth	10,369.5	8,923.8
Growth & Income	19,962.7	9,438.6
Precious Metals	8,745.5	4,261.6
International	3,872.7	1,277.3
Global Equity	561.3	173.9
Income-equity	2,722.0	1,254.6
Option/Income	288.5	291.8
Flexible Portfolio	385.7	233.2
Balanced	741.0	384.1
Income-mixed	1,173.5	771.0
Income-bond	1,898.0	1,451.0
U.S. Government Income	4,013.3	3,660.5
Ginnie Mae	1,988.2	1,318.9
Global Bond	437.9	605.0
Corporate Bond	1,595.4	1,649.8
High-yield Bond	3,397.7	4,364.2
Long-term Municipal Bond	12,569.0	8,670.1
State Municipal Bond, Long-term	3,903.2	3,076.6
Short-term Municipal Bond	12,244.7R	6,543.9
State Municipal Bond, Short-term	3,175.4	2,563.3
Money Market	83,402.4R	55,526.2

R--Revised

Redemptions Due to Exchanges
by Investment Objective
1987-1988
(millions of dollars)

Investment Objective	1987	1988
Aggressive Growth	$30,544.0	$19,403.4
Growth	11,610.3	10,568.5
Growth & Income	20,888.9	11,939.9
Precious Metals	8,423.6	4,428.0
International	6,039.5	1,923.8
Global Equity	747.8	472.4
Income-equity	3,499.9	1,791.6
Option/Income	715.5	586.6
Flexible Portfolio	189.5	310.9
Balanced	958.2	722.9
Income-mixed	1,605.0	860.8
Income-bond	2,182.1	1,223.4
U.S. Government Income	8,908.6	4,498.2
Ginnie Mae	4,806.3	2,020.4
Global Bond	348.6	613.7
Corporate Bond	1,978.6	1,697.4
High-yield Bond	5,172.7	3,484.0
Long-term Municipal Bond	17,485.9	8,553.5
State Municipal Bond, Long-term	6,214.5	3,012.8
Short-term Municipal Bond	9,737.0	6,757.4
State Municipal Bond, Short-term	1,765.6	1,718.8
Money Market	63,630.8R	47,711.9

R--Revised

Net Sales Due to Exchanges by Investment Objective
1987-1988
(millions of dollars)

Investment Objective	1987	1988
Aggressive Growth	$(2,276.5)	$(1,547.8)
Growth	(1,240.8)	(1,644.7)
Growth & Income	(926.2)	(2,501.3)
Precious Metals	321.9	(166.4)
International	(2,166.9)	(646.5)
Global Equity	(186.4)	(298.5)
Income-equity	(777.9)	(537.0)
Option/Income	(427.0)	(294.8)
Flexible Portfolio	196.2	(77.7)
Balanced	(217.2)	(338.8)
Income-mixed	(431.5)	(89.8)
Income-bond	(284.1)	227.6
U.S. Government Income	(4,895.3)	(837.8)
Ginnie Mae	(2,818.1)	(701.5)
Global Bond	89.3	(8.6)
Corporate Bond	(383.3)	(47.5)
High-yield Bond	(1,775.0)	880.2
Long-term Municipal Bond	(4,916.9)	116.6
State Municipal Bond, Long-term	(2,311.3)	63.8
Short-term Municipal Bond	2,507.7R	(213.4)
State Municipal Bond, Short-term	1,409.9	844.5
Money Market	19,771.8R	7,814.3

R--Revised

IRA Assets and Accounts by Investment Objective Yearend 1988

Investment Objective	Assets		Accounts	
	Millions of Dollars	Percent	Number (thousands)	Percent
Aggressive Growth	$8,641.7	10.0%	1,825.4	11.7%
Growth	8,847.4	10.3	1,818.5	11.6
Growth & Income	12,276.8	14.3	2,180.3	13.9
Precious Metals	754.4	0.9	278.3	1.8
International	1,165.9	1.4	301.5	1.9
Global Equity	2,469.1	2.9	463.9	3.0
Income-equity	4,252.3	4.9	800.2	5.1
Option/Income	823.0	1.0	139.2	0.9
Flexible Portfolio	891.6	1.0	174.0	1.1
Balanced	1,426.6	1.7	266.7	1.7
Income-mixed	1,303.1	1.5	185.6	1.2
Income-bond	1,454.0	1.7	177.4	1.1
U.S. Government Income	11,751.1	13.6	1,347.8	8.6
Ginnie Mae	4,279.7	5.0	591.5	3.8
Global Bond	137.2	0.2	23.2	0.2
Corporate Bond	1,934.1	2.2	237.7	1.5
High-yield Bond	6,200.1	7.2	788.6	5.0
Money Market	17,384.6	20.2	4,050.9	25.9
Total	**$85,992.7**	**100.0%**	**15,650.7**	**100.0%**

Self-employed Retirement Plan Assets and Accounts by Investment Objective Yearend 1988

Investment Objective	Assets		Accounts	
	Millions of Dollars	Percent	Number (Thousands)	Percent
Aggressive Growth	$979.8	9.1%	77.4	9.6%
Growth	1,593.1	14.8	73.2	9.0
Growth & Income	1,765.2	16.3	79.6	9.8
Precious Metals	67.3	0.6	8.9	1.1
International	112.2	1.0	10.2	1.3
Global Equity	168.4	1.6	8.8	1.1
Income-equity	396.4	3.7	25.5	3.2
Option/Income	29.9	0.3	1.7	0.2
Flexible Portfolio	97.2	0.9	6.8	0.8
Balanced	168.2	1.6	10.6	1.3
Income-mixed	179.5	1.7	12.3	1.5
Income-bond	187.0	1.7	6.6	0.8
U.S. Government Income	340.2	3.1	24.8	3.1
Ginnie Mae	403.9	3.7	26.4	3.3
Global Bond	15.0	0.1	1.3	0.2
Corporate Bond	441.3	4.1	18.7	2.3
High-yield Bond	538.5	5.0	32.8	4.0
Money Market	3,314.1	30.7	384.4	47.4
Total	**$10,797.2**	**100.0%**	**810.0**	**100.0%**

An Overview: Fiduciary, Business, and Institutional Investors in Equity, Bond, and Income Funds

Year	Reporting Companies' Assets (millions)	Percent Assets of Total Members' Assets	Reported Institutional Accounts in Force	Reported Value of Holdings (millions)	Reported Institutional Holdings as a Percent of Total Net Assets
1970	$32,631.1	68.5%	1,071,243	$6,174.0	18.9%
1972	44,696.4	74.7	1,119,243	8,906.9	19.9
1974	26,981.4	75.4	1,440,533	7,116.1	26.4
1976	39,342.2	77.3	1,346,490	10,719.7	27.2
1978	37,043.3	82.4	1,258,996	9,590.5	25.9
1980	45,763.2	78.4	1,023,101	12,855.9	28.1
1981	48,364.0	87.6	771,585	11,405.3	23.6
1982	66,569.2	86.7	953,483	16,232.7	24.4
1983	99,911.0	88.0	1,327,304	23,314.8	23.8
1984	126,354.1	92.1	1,415,021	30,304.3	24.0
1985	213,821.7	85.0	2,066,265	52,697.9	24.6
1986	359,355.4	84.7	4,072,491	102,063.3	28.4
1987	373,834.2	82.4	4,068,402	97,091.5	21.4
1988	395,038.8	92.5	5,809,625	99,644.8	21.1

Note: *Prior to 1981, Keogh and IRA figures are included in institutional holdings. Institutional holdings as a percent of assets of reporting companies are slightly understated prior to 1974 due to limited reporting of Keogh information. Reported institutional accounts and value of holdings for 1981 and 1982 were used to derive universe estimates shown in the following tables which present institutional data in greater detail. The 1981 figures were revised to exclude Keogh and IRA. In the 1980 figures, Keogh and IRA accounted for about 30 percent of institutional accounts and 23 percent of institutional assets.*

Number of Accounts of Fiduciary, Business, and Institutional Investors in Equity, Bond, and Income Funds

	1985R	1986R	1987R	1988
Fiduciaries (Banks and Individuals Serving as Trustees, Guardians, and Administrators)	**1,331,093**	**2,535,496**	**2,448,891**	**2,230,840**
Business Corporations	119,052	168,000	166,221	138,245
Retirement Plans	1,056,969	1,300,158	1,610,626	1,643,657
Insurance Companies and Other Financial Institutions	25,234	50,983	73,450	65,941
Unions	770	1,590	2,563	1,309
Total Business Organizations	**1,202,025**	**1,520,731**	**1,852,860**	**1,849,152**
Churches and Religious Organizations	11,627	16,501	18,887	18,281
Fraternal, Welfare, and Other Public Associations	8,119	13,972	11,141	12,445
Hospitals, Sanitariums, Orphanages, etc.	2,699	7,242	5,382	3,489
Schools and Colleges	4,891	6,474	6,742	6,332
Foundations	4,657	5,213	16,769	6,843
Total Institutions and Foundations	**31,993**	**49,402**	**58,921**	**47,390**
Other Institutional Investors Not Classified (a)	**67,330**	**209,315**	**198,053**	**371,737**
Total	**2,632,441**	**4,314,944**	**4,558,725**	**4,499,119**

(a) Includes institutional accounts which do not fall under other classifications and those for which no determination of classification can be made.

Note: Reporters of institutional data represented 83.3% of total shareholder accounts in 1985, 82.6% in 1986, 81.8% in 1987, and 81.8% in 1988. The figures shown above are universe-estimated based on those reports.

R–Revised. Historical data series have been revised to reflect a more accurate method of identifying multiple service accounts.

Number of Accounts of Fiduciary, Business, and Institutional Investors in Money Market Funds

	1985R	1986R	1987R	1988
Fiduciaries (Banks and Individuals Serving as Trustees, Guardians, and Administrators)	**752,133**	**796,988**	**1,033,504**	**943,094**
Business Corporations	247,864	270,265	257,300	236,934
Retirement Plans	379,406	371,839	447,349	436,304
Insurance Companies and Other Financial Institutions	20,745	25,970	23,904	25,731
Unions	953	3,843	9,057	3,218
Total Business Organizations	**648,968**	**671,917**	**737,610**	**702,187**
Churches and Religious Organizations	16,223	15,147	14,862	13,833
Fraternal, Welfare, and Other Public Associations	10,808	15,259	13,361	12,343
Hospitals, Sanitariums, Orphanages, etc.	4,875	4,391	5,248	2,997
Schools and Colleges	6,133	6,337	5,723	3,623
Foundations	2,531	2,961	1,694	5,023
Total Institutions and Foundations	**40,570**	**44,095**	**40,888**	**37,819**
Other Institutional Investors Not Classified (a)	**45,184**	**244,187**	**73,523**	**51,157**
Total	**1,486,855**	**1,757,187**	**1,885,525**	**1,734,257**

(a) Includes institutional accounts which do not fall under other classifications and those for which no determination of classification can be made.

Note: Reporters of institutional data represented 61.0% of total shareholder accounts in 1985, 53.3% in 1986, 55.0% in 1987, and 53.1% in 1988.

R--Revised. Historical data series have been revised to reflect a more accurate method of identifying multiple service accounts.

Number of Accounts of Fiduciary, Business, and Institutional Investors in Money Market Funds by Type of Fund

	General Purpose		Broker/Dealer		Institutional	
	1987R	1988	1987R	1988	1987R	1988
Fiduciaries (Banks and Individuals Serving as Trustees, Guardians, and Administrators)	**433,899**	**349,500**	**513,443**	**497,763**	**86,162**	**95,831**
Business Corporations	112,596	97,898	137,092	131,559	7,612	7,477
Retirement Plans	223,167	306,308	221,197	126,466	2,985	3,530
Insurance Companies and Other Financial Institutions	8,345	12,738	14,824	10,036	735	2,957
Unions	582	2,214	8,454	749	21	255
Total Business Organizations	**344,690**	**419,158**	**381,567**	**268,810**	**11,353**	**14,219**
Churches and Religious Organizations	8,217	7,627	6,430	5,845	215	361
Fraternal, Welfare, and Other Public Associations	6,638	7,727	6,126	4,050	597	566
Hospitals, Sanitariums, Orphanages, etc.	1,918	1,082	3,065	1,582	265	333
Schools and Colleges	2,682	1,681	2,866	1,617	175	325
Foundations	1,157	1,214	514	1,884	23	1,925
Total Institutions and Foundations	**20,612**	**19,331**	**19,001**	**14,978**	**1,275**	**3,510**
Other Institutional Investors Not Classified (a)	**25,131**	**31,409**	**47,980**	**17,690**	**412**	**2,058**
Total	**824,332**	**819,398**	**961,991**	**799,241**	**99,202**	**115,618**

(a) Includes institutional accounts which do not fall under other classifications and those for which no determination of classification can be made.

R--Revised. Historical data series have been revised to reflect a more accurate method of identifying multiple service accounts.

Number of Accounts of Fiduciary, Business, and Institutional Investors in Short-term Municipal Bond Funds

	1985R	1986R	1987R	1988
Fiduciaries (Banks and Individuals Serving as Trustees, Guardians, and Administrators)	**37,611**	**48,449**	**77,832**	**56,354**
Business Corporations	9,576	10,616	10,748	9,817
Retirement Plans	409	498	2,058	1,422
Insurance Companies and Other Financial Institutions	1,182	2,153	998	1,854
Unions	7	4	489	15
Total Business Organizations	**11,174**	**13,271**	**14,293**	**13,108**
Churches and Religious Organizations	13	26	28	41
Fraternal, Welfare, and Other Public Associations	53	99	466	231
Hospitals, Sanitariums, Orphanages, etc.	388	88	42	32
Schools and Colleges	17	44	59	40
Foundations	2	4	11	28
Total Institutions and Foundations	**473**	**261**	**606**	**372**
Other Institutional Investors Not Classified (a)	**2,250**	**6,262**	**3,423**	**5,007**
Total	**51,508**	**68,243**	**96,154**	**74,841**

(a) Includes institutional accounts which do not fall under other classifications and those for which no determination of classification can be made.

Note: Short-term municipal bond fund reporters represented 59.7% of total shareholder accounts in 1985, 57.9% in 1986, 71.4% in 1987, and 73.2% in 1988.

R—Revised. Historical data series have been revised to reflect a more accurate method of identifying multiple service accounts.

Assets of Fiduciary, Business, and Institutional Investors in Equity, Bond, and Income Funds

(millions of dollars)

	1985R	1986	1987R	1988
Fiduciaries (Banks and Individuals Serving as Trustees, Guardians, and Administrators)	**$22,657.5**	**$51,076.1**	**$51,976.4**	**$46,496.1**
Business Corporations	10,798.8	15,675.8	12,817.6	10,627.1
Retirement Plans	19,050.7	26,431.6	28,974.3	31,165.6
Insurance Companies and Other Financial Institutions	3,513.5	14,460.1	12,099.2	18,474.1
Unions	72.4	202.7	352.7	147.6
Total Business Organizations	**$33,435.4**	**$56,770.2**	**$54,243.8**	**$60,414.4**
Churches and Religious Organizations	593.8	853.6	1,320.1	801.4
Fraternal, Welfare, and Other Public Associations	477.3	1,186.9	974.2	940.7
Hospitals, Sanitariums, Orphanages, etc.	237.9	497.7	473.4	360.1
Schools and Colleges	376.1	705.7	922.9	658.2
Foundations	265.8	467.7	703.9	415.9
Total Institutions and Foundations	**$1,950.9**	**$3,711.5**	**$4,394.5**	**$3,176.2**
Other Institutional Investors Not Classified (a)	**$3,250.3**	**$5,407.1**	**$6,467.7**	**$10,034.8**
Total	**$61,294.1**	**$116,964.9**	**$117,082.4**	**$120,121.6**

(a) Includes institutional accounts which do not fall under other classifications and those for which no determination of classification can be made.

Note: Reporters of institutional data represented 85.0% of total net assets in 1985, 84.7% in 1986, 82.4% in 1987, and 83.6% in 1988. The figures shown above are universe estimated based on those reports.

R—Revised

Assets of Fiduciary, Business, and Institutional Investors in Money Market Funds

(millions of dollars)

	1985	1986	1987R	1988
Fiduciaries (Banks and Individuals Serving as Trustees, Guardians, and Administrators)	**$52,455.8**	**$61,292.4**	**$75,238.2**	**$73,165.0**
Business Corporations	$12,817.4	14,230.7	15,464.7	13,058.4
Retirement Plans	9,078.3	13,116.2	11,302.8	12,838.7
Insurance Companies and Other Financial Institutions	7,396.7	7,548.7	6,320.6	6,169.2
Unions	81.8	514.6	466.6	235.1
Total Business Organizations	**$29,374.2**	**$35,410.2**	**$33,554.7**	**$32,301.4**
Churches and Religious Organizations	540.0	537.6	523.3	536.6
Fraternal, Welfare, and Other Public Associations	377.6	749.3	903.3	984.2
Hospitals, Sanitariums, Orphanages, etc.	444.8	369.8	495.7	314.5
Schools and Colleges	291.2	431.3	552.8	313.5
Foundations	278.9	222.7	90.8	370.3
Total Institutions and Foundations	**$1,932.5**	**$2,310.7**	**$2,565.9**	**$2,519.1**
Other Institutional Investors Not Classified (a)	**$5,939.5**	**$4,222.5**	**$2,981.2**	**$9,040.3**
Total	**$89,702.0**	**$103,235.8**	**$114,340.0**	**$117,025.8**

(a) Includes institutional accounts which do not fall under other classifications and those for which no determination of classification can be made.

Note: Reporters of institutional data represented 62.4% of net assets in 1985, 53.5% in 1986, 61.1% in 1987, and 69.2% in 1988. The figures shown above are universe estimated based on those reports.

R—Revised

Assets of Fiduciary, Business, and Institutional Investors in Money Market Funds by Type of Fund

(millions of dollars)

	General Purpose		Broker/Dealer		Institutional	
	1987R	1988	1987R	1988	1987R	1988
Fiduciaries (Banks and Individuals Serving as Trustees, Guardians, and Administrators)	**$10,405.4**	**$11,201.2**	**$6,917.4**	**$7,654.5**	**$57,915.4**	**$54,309.3**
Business Corporations	6,321.1	4,602.1	5,287.2	4,800.1	3,856.4	3,656.3
Retirement Plans	5,836.4	8,532.6	5,154.0	3,874.3	312.4	431.7
Insurance Companies and Other Financial Institutions	3,183.1	3,203.6	1,501.1	496.8	1,636.3	2,468.7
Unions	62.1	102.0	390.1	52.7	14.5	80.4
Total Business Organizations	**$15,402.7**	**$16,440.3**	**$12,332.4**	**$9,223.9**	**$5,819.6**	**$6,637.1**
Churches and Religious Organizations	237.2	229.5	258.4	211.9	27.7	95.2
Fraternal, Welfare, and Other Public Associations	409.5	415.1	259.0	220.0	234.9	349.1
Hospitals, Sanitariums, Orphanages, etc.	168.6	79.0	165.8	96.6	161.4	138.8
Schools and Colleges	157.0	109.4	314.4	89.0	81.4	115.1
Foundations	60.1	52.9	14.6	131.0	16.0	186.4
Total Institutions and Foundations	**$1,032.4**	**$885.9**	**$1,012.2**	**$748.5**	**$521.4**	**$884.6**
Other Institutional Investors Not Classified (a)	**$987.1**	**$1,373.1**	**$1,783.5**	**$1,499.8**	**$210.6**	**$6,167.5**
Total	**$27,827.6**	**$29,900.5**	**$22,045.6**	**$19,126.7**	**$64,467.0**	**$67,998.6**

(a) Includes institutional assets which do not fall under other classifications and those for which no determination of classification can be made.

R–Revised

Assets of Fiduciary, Business, and Institutional Investors in Short-term Municipal Bond Funds

(millions of dollars)

	1985	1986	1987R	1988
Fiduciaries (Banks and Individuals Serving as Trustees, Guardians, and Administrators)	**$12,519.4**	**$25,549.5**	**$20,989.1**	**$18,303.7**
Business Corporations	1,702.8	3,891.3	3,480.3	2,590.5
Retirement Plans	8.0	127.2	91.6	115.4
Insurance Companies and Other Financial Institutions	1,576.8	2,465.6	592.4	794.1
Unions	0.2	25.5	198.1	20.0
Total Business Organizations	**$3,287.8**	**$6,509.6**	**$4,362.4**	**$3,520.0**
Churches and Religious Organizations	0.7	12.7	1.8	19.9
Fraternal, Welfare, and Other Public Associations	2.3	14.3	58.4	54.9
Hospitals, Sanitariums, Orphanages, etc.	1.1	2.9	2.1	24.8
Schools and Colleges	5.2	2.7	12.0	52.0
Foundations	0.0	0.1	0.1	32.2
Total Institutions and Foundations	**$9.3**	**$32.7**	**$74.4**	**$183.8**
Other Institutional Investors Not Classified (a)	**$727.6**	**$572.6**	**$643.0**	**$2,808.7**
Total	**$16,544.1**	**$32,664.4**	**$26,068.9**	**$24,816.2**

(a) Includes institutional total net assets which do not fall under other classifications and those for which no determination of classification can be made.

Note: Short-term municipal bond fund reporters represented 65.5% of total net assets in 1985, 61.5% in 1986, 69.4% in 1987, and 58.5% in 1988.

R--Revised

Assets of Major Institutions and Financial Intermediaries

(millions of dollars)

	1983	1984	1985	1986	1987	1988
Depository Institutions						
Commercial Banks	$2,093,800	$2,264,800	$2,483,800	$2,597,700	$2,721,400	$3,030,800
Credit Unions (a)	81,961	93,036	118,010	147,726R	183,600	173,276(b)
Mutual Savings Banks	193,535	203,898	216,776	236,866R	259,643R	257,127(c)
Savings & Loan Associations	838,386(d)	1,002,047(d)	1,080,649(d)	1,163,851R	1,250,855R	1,333,233(c)
Life Insurance	**$654,948**	**$722,979**	**$825,901**	**$937,551**	**$1,044,459**	**$1,131,179**
Investment Institutions						
Bank Administered Trusts (e)	$762,800	$801,661	$945,448	$1,065,324	$1,085,078	NA
Closed-end Investment Companies	NA	6,051	7,618	12,915	21,390	$39,493
Mutual Funds (f)	292,985	370,680	495,498	716,308	769,900	810,300

(a) Includes only federal or federally insured state credit unions serving natural persons.
(b) As of July 1988.
(c) As of October 1988.
(d) Includes FSLIC-insured institutions.
(e) Reflects only discretionary trusts and agencies.
(f) Includes Short-term Funds.
NA Not available
R--Revised

Index

More Information on Mutual Funds

With the exception of the Fact Book and Guide, single copies of our brochures are available without charge to the general public. Please use the order form on the back of this page to request brochures, the Guide, or additional copies of the Fact Book. For information on volume quantities, contact the Investment Company Institute, 1600 M Street, NW, Suite 600, Washington, DC 20036, 202/955-3534.

What Is a Mutual Fund?
8 FUNDamentals
This concise, illustrated leaflet opens out to reveal all eight key features of a mutual fund investment. Includes a table showing how to read mutual fund share quotes and a chart illustrating the risk/return tradeoff.

A Translation: Turning Investment-ese into Investment Ease
This brochure acts as interpreter for the investor who is trying to penetrate the jargon of the financial world. A step-by-step explanation of the advantages of mutual funds helps the reader determine investment priorities and how to attain them.

Discipline. It Can't Really Be Good for You, Can It?
Dollar-cost averaging, the strategy of buying more when the price of mutual fund shares is low and buying less when the price is high, is explained in this colorful leaflet. Shows how dollar-cost averaging works when the market fluctuates, declines, and rises.

Planning for College? The Mutual Fund Advantage Becomes a Parent
The value of a college education is well-known. This brochure offers practical insights to those preparing to meet the rising costs of a college education...and outlines the major advantages of mutual funds in meeting those costs. Information on the latest tax rules for minors is included.

Money Market Mutual Funds--A Part of Every Financial Plan
In easy-to-understand language, this brochure explores money market funds--an investment that changed the way Americans handle their money. Explains why millions of Americans looking for safety, liquidity, and yield turn to money market funds.

Mutual Fund Fact Book
Annually updated facts and figures on the U.S. mutual fund industry, including trends in sales, assets, and performance. Outlines history and growth of the fund industry, its policies, operations, regulation, services, and shareholders.
120 pages   *$9.95 each*

Guide to Mutual Funds (includes directory of funds)
In addition to fund names, addresses, and telephone numbers (many toll-free), the guide lists each fund's assets, initial and subsequent investment requirements, the year it began, where to buy shares, and other pertinent details. The funds are categorized by their investment objectives. An introductory text serves as a "short course" in mutual fund investing.
180 pages   *$2.00 each*

Payment must accompany orders for the Fact Book and the Guide to Mutual Funds.

Speaker Referral Service
The Institute can help you find a leading mutual fund executive to address your group, class, or meeting. In a generic, educational presentation, your group can learn the basics of mutual fund investing, the types and benefits of funds, the factors to consider when selecting a fund, and more. Speakers are available in most areas of the country. Call Stephanie Brown at 202/955-3536 for more information.
No charge

The Institute also offers a variety of films, videos, and slides on mutual funds.
Call 202/955-3534 or check the box below for more information.

Order Form

Brochures and Publications

Note: Materials are available to schools, clubs, and libraries without cost. Payment must
accompany orders for Fact Books and the Guide to Mutual Funds. Please allow three weeks
for delivery.

	Unit Cost	Quantity	Total
What Is a Mutual Fund? 8 FUNDamentals	free		free
A Translation: Turning Investment-ese into Investment Ease	free		free
Discipline. It Can't Really Be Good for You, Can It?	free		free
Planning for College	free		free
Money Market Mutual Funds-- A Part of Every Financial Plan	free		free
Mutual Fund Fact Book (prepay)	$ 9.95		
Guide to Mutual Funds (prepay)	$ 2.00		
Total Cost			

☐ Yes! I would like more information about mutual funds.
Please send me the publications catalog.

Please print clearly and return order form and check to:
Publication Orders, Investment Company Institute, 1600 M Street, NW, Suite 600
Washington, DC 20036.

Name

Title

Company

*Street Address

City   State   Zip

Telephone

*Volume quantities will be shipped UPS. Please do not use a post office box number or rural
route address for volume quantities. UPS will not deliver to these addresses.